"Quite simply the best guide I've read for the stage struck hopeful who wants to turn pro. . . . At graduating ceremonies of drama schools and professional acting programs, I propose instead of diplomas they hand out Robert Cohen's book."

RAY DEMATTIS, *Regional Theatre Directory 1995–96*

"A must for those who want to understand the biz."

DAVI NAPOLEON, *Theatre Week*, March 18, 1996

"The much-praised book is as successful and valuable as ever . . . [and] fully exposes the aspiring actor to the 'raw facts' of the business."

JEFFREY SCOTT ELWELL, *Theatre Journal*, December 1990

"This is the book that every mother should stick in her son's or daughter's bag next to the chocolate chip cookies as she packs them off from Fort Wayne on their way to the wicked city—on either coast—to be an actor (or just off to college to major in the arts). . . . Cohen . . . is eminently businesslike and realistic without being unnecessarily negative, and his advice is sound."

JILL CHARLES, *Regional Theatre Directory 1989–90*

"The most straightforward, accurate, and honest description of what the acting business is like in the United States and what it takes to break into it. An absolute must."

ROGER ELLIS, *An Audition Handbook for Student Actors*

"An invaluable labor on Mr. Cohen's part."

AUSTIN PENDLETON, *Yale Theatre*

"Packed with precise and detailed information on all the things which the aspiring actor doesn't know about and should. It is an invaluable book."

JOHN HARROP, *Educational Theatre Journal*

"All you ever needed to know (but were afraid to ask) about breaking into the acting business."

OLGA MAYNARD, *After Dark*

"Cohen performs a magnificent service both to aspiring actors and to the theatre."

ERIC FORSYTHE, *Dartmouth Alumni Magazine*

"Clearly put information and practical advice. An excellent guide to the business of acting professionally in the United States."

*Hollywood Reporter*

# ACTING
## *Professionally*

RAW FACTS ABOUT
CAREERS IN ACTING

FIFTH EDITION

Robert Cohen

*University of California, Irvine*

Mayfield Publishing Company
Mountain View, California
London • Toronto

**Library of Congress Cataloging-in-Publication Data**
Cohen, Robert
    Acting professionally : raw facts about careers in acting / Robert Cohen. — 5th ed.
        p.   cm.
    Includes bibliographical references and index.
    ISBN 1-55934-941-7
    1. Acting—Vocational guidance—United States.   I. Title.
PN2055.C57   1997
792'.028'02373—dc21                                                    97-14559
                                                                        CIP

Manufactured in the United States of America
10   9   8   7   6   5   4   3

Mayfield Publishing Company
1280 Villa Street
Mountain View, California 94041

Sponsoring editor, Janet M. Beatty; production editor, Carla L. White; manuscript editor, Mark Gallaher; design manager, Jean Mailander; art editor, Amy Folden; manufacturing manager, Randy Hurst. The text was set in 10/12 New Baskerville by TBH Typecast and printed on 50# Ecolocote by Malloy Lithographing, Inc.

# Preface

It amazes me to realize that a quarter-century has passed—quite eventfully, I must say—since I first wrote *Acting Professionally*. In that time just about everything in the acting business has changed. There are twice as many television broadcast networks as when I wrote the first edition, and at least ten times the number of nonprofit theatres. There are professional performing opportunities on media not even thought of in previous decades, including cable television, rental videocassettes, corporate videos, and interactive CD-ROMs. Dinner theatre has both come and (largely) gone, but cruise ships and Shakespearean festivals have virtually taken off as major talent employers.

And there's been an international conglomeratization of the entire entertainment industry, to the extent that a few world-wide enterprises—Disney/Capital Cities/ABC, Time/Warner/Turner, News Corp/Fox, and Westinghouse/CBS—virtually write (or at least underwrite) the rules of the acting profession for stage, film, and TV.

The money from all this has just about gone through the roof. What was a million dollar Broadway musical in the 60s can now cost close to $15 million. Major films now average $60 million a pop; James Cameron's *Titanic* came in at a reputed $200 million. Salaries of the very top film stars, which were falling off their $1 million peak when I wrote the first edition, are now $20 million and more for at least a half dozen stars, with Bruce Willis commanding a reported $35 million for his fourth *Die Hard* extravaganza.

And yet the words of past Screen Actors Guild president William Shallert are as true today as they've ever been, so I repeat them here: "Making a living as an actor is like trying to cross a rapidly rushing river stepping from one slowly sinking rock to another slowly sinking rock." And Shallert was talking about film actors. For stage actors the river is deeper and the rocks are sinking even more quickly.

When I first wrote it, this book was quite a novelty: No such book existed at the time, apart from a slim tome entitled *Turn On To Stardom*—a would-be career guide as relentlessly optimistic as it was naively well-meaning. Beginning actors, in those days, were almost wholly in the dark about the mysteries of unions, agents, salaries, and the overall job market. I remember the actors in my Yale Drama School class literally begging the faculty to explain the steps by which they could turn their M.F.A. diplomas into AEA (that's Actors Equity Association) contracts. And the faculty, for the most part, didn't have the foggiest idea. Well, this has changed most of all. Today, show business is everybody's business. Network television programs like *Entertainment Tonight*, *Access Hollywood*, and *Showbiz Today* report every in and out of the acting business on a daily basis. Professional trade journals like *Variety* and *Hollywood Reporter* are supplemented with mass-market (but serious) fan magazines like *Entertainment Weekly* and *Premiere*. And the professional trades themselves—not just *Variety* but also *Back Stage, Billboard*, and *Drama-Logue*—can increasingly be found at ordinary suburban newsstands in greater metropolitan areas. The news of show business has become a show business itself. Regular city newspapers around the country print cinema box office statistics and Neilson TV ratings weekly, plus detailed articles on actor hirings, firings, hospitalizations, and salary negotiations. Mass-market magazines such as *People, Us,* and *Vanity Fair* are at least half-filled every issue with actor interviews, detailing every aspect—fiscal and artistic—of the "biz." TV presents actors acting from daytime to prime time, and then shows actors talking about their acting in the talk shows that follow long into the night—and the following morning.

It's not surprising, therefore, that today there's a virtual library of books on the same subject as this one. Many of them, indeed, have the same table of contents you see here. And almost all of them—graced with the personal experiences of their authors—are helpful and worth reading; several are cited in the bibliography.

Plus, there are even more specialized texts today devoted to individual topics in this business: whole books, for example, on acting in commercials, acting in industrials, acting in Chicago, working in voice-overs, preparing resumes, choosing agents, getting your kids an agent, and so forth. There is even a book on getting your *pet* into show biz. Many of these books are listed in the appendix at the back of this book, and many new ones will have appeared by the time you are reading this. You can easily spend a whole day looking over the field simply by standing in front of the relevant shelves of the Drama Book Shop in New York or the Samuel French Theatre Book Shop in Los Angeles— or any of the theatre book shops that have recently appeared in Seattle, Chicago, Toronto, and other North American cities. The work situation of an actor is no longer a mystery to anyone who's the slightest bit interested.

I'm very happy to find that this book still has its place, however. It remains, true to its continuing subtitle, the "raw facts" about acting careers. It is a book of research as much as a book of advice: research that takes place on both coasts and in the theatre centers between. It is objective: I have no particular axe to grind (on this subject, anyway), and no special story of my own to tell. Acting remains for me a magnificent occupation for those who get to do it. It is a joy, an exaltation, and a profound learning experience: about yourself and about human life around you. To a great many it is both an art and a passion. It is a chance to work hard, and to play hard and—when all comes together in a great performance—to ring the bells of a very special church. I love and admire actors—and the profession they profess. But I also acknowledge that it's probably the most difficult way to make a living you could find. And I must share what I acknowledge.

What follows, then, is both information—the "raw facts" which, indeed, are getting even a little rawer—and some reasonable conclusions you might draw therefrom. The "advice" presented in these pages is not merely my own, but the very broad and very persuasive consensus of those with whom I talk almost every day of my life: actors, directors, agents, casting directors, and producers in what we should call "the acting business."

## WHAT'S NEW?

This edition takes into account the burgeoning technological revolution, which has brought CD-ROMs and the Internet into the resource pool for actors and for the people who cast them. I have also expanded the film/television/West Coast sections a bit, since the opportunities in acting are growing faster in these areas, while stage opportunities remain relatively stable. (Indeed, the number of Screen Actors Guild members has increased by more than 15,000—by 21%—since the previous edition of this book, while the number of Actors Equity Association members—who work in live theatre—has actually declined. Also somewhat alarming is the disappearance on the East Coast of three major stage-oriented periodicals—*Theatre Week, Show Business,* and, at least temporarily, *Player's Guide*—while comparable West Coast actor publications, like *Back Stage West* and *Drama-Logue,* are expanding their size and readerships.) Conversely, however, I have somewhat expanded the section on regional theatre opportunities and resources, and provided some new listings for Chicago and Seattle. Everything in the book, of course, has been entirely updated, and about two-thirds of the text has been wholly rewritten to include these changes as seamlessly as possible.

I've also added a brief section on "Getting the *Second* Job." It's a problem I've grown increasingly interested in as my own graduates get further along in their careers. Getting the second job turns out to be quite a bit different than getting the first—and, perhaps surprisingly to some, it is not necessarily easier. I hope this section proves to be a useful and interesting one.

A final update: The Screen Actors Guild (SAG) and the American Federation of Television and Radio Artists (AFTRA) have been talking about a merger for more than thirty years; indeed, such a possible merger was noted in the first edition of this book a generation ago. Now it finally appears to be imminent. But it's not yet official, and in no case will such a merger be in place before this book hits the stands. So I have retained discussion of both unions in this edition, together with the likely results of a merged SAG/AFTRA. As the merged union will carry over all current contracts, the proposed merger should have no significant implications for entry-level film/TV actors, at least for the next few years. But it will be a factor to be reckoned with in the future.

## ACKNOWLEDGMENTS

One of the great pleasures I've had in teaching acting for more than thirty years is the continuing rapport I enjoy with my former students, a large number of whom now populate the theatre professions. To many of them I have turned, during the preparation of each of the five editions of this book, for current counsel on the vagaries of the ever-changing situation of the professional actor. Their assistance has been professionally invaluable, as well as personally gratifying in the extreme. Nearly a hundred of these former students have been acknowledged in previous editions; for the present version, I have turned to three in particular who have been tremendously helpful: Jeff Greenberg, casting director for *Frasier, Cheers, Wings, Early Edition, Father of the Bride II,* and many others; James Calleri, a New York agent and stage producer, and now casting director for Playwrights Horizons, films, and ABC Television (*NYPD Blues*); and Bruce Bouchard, formerly Artistic Director of the Capital Repertory Theatre in Albany, New York, and currently co-president of Gold/Bouchard Productions in Hollywood. Plus, I would like to acknowledge the contributions of those former students who are now professional actors, and who have responded to my inquiries for this edition, namely, Brian Thompson, Kelly Perrine, Rebecca Clark, Maura Vincent, Jon Lovitz, Ayre Gross, Maire Mansouri, Bob Gunton, Jeff Meek, Sarah Richardson, Luck Hari, Joel Forsythe, Kevin Mahoney, Linda Alper, Tyler Layton,

Michael Sabatino, Josh Finkel, John Shepard, Mark Hutter, Gary Graham, Mikael Salazar, Nicholas Walker, Jennifer Roszell, Mark Booher, Ann Hamilton, Kitty Balay-Genge, Joan Stuart-Morris, Henry Leyva, and Joel Goldes. To each and all, for your wise counsel and general advice, many thanks.

I'd also like to thank the reviewers who pored through the manuscript for this edition and provided valuable insights: James Calleri, Playwrights Horizons; Bruce Cromer, Wright State University; Richard Jennings, University of South Carolina; Richard Klautsch, Boise State University; and Thomas Mills, *Back Stage West.*

A final note: "Hollywood," where used in this book other than in written addresses, does not necessarily correlate to the geographical boundaries of the Los Angeles district of that name. More generally, "Hollywood" is used to refer to the world of film and television production that takes place in the greater Los Angeles area, which may mean Studio City, University City, Culver City, Burbank, Beverly Hills, Century City, or even Hollywood itself. "Hollywood" is not a city; it is a business, a culture, a state of mind. Similarly, "New York," as used in this book, rarely refers to any of the seven boroughs of that city outside of Manhattan.

# Contents

# Chapter 1

# The Way It Is

Let's face it: Acting is fun. Millions of people do it for free. And millions more want to do it for their living.

And why not? At the top, acting is one of the most sublime activities of the human species. Imagine playing Hamlet, or Hedda, or Rocky XII to cheering audiences. Imagine the amazement and envy of your friends. Imagine going head to head with Jay Leno or Dave Letterman, sharing some juicy gossip from the set, or putting down your enemies (the former professor who said you'd never make it?) with a wry riposte. Imagine world tours, fawning politicians, ardent groupies. Love scenes with world-renowned heartthrobs played in exotic locations. Running down the aisle to pick up your Tony or Oscar in front of millions of viewers worldwide, and the parties that follow. Imagine addressing the Democratic National Convention in prime time, or delivering the State of the Union address to Congress as the reigning U.S. President. Christopher Reeve and Ronald Reagan did it, why shouldn't you? As the late Jimmy Durante used to say, "Everybody wants to get into the act!" And, again, why not?

Actors, as you know, make a ton of money these days. Mel Gibson, Jim Carrey, Sylvester Stallone, Robin Williams, Jack Nicholson, and the Toms Cruise and Hanks all command a reported $20 million per film or more. Arnold Schwarzenegger and Bruce Willis are in the $30–$35 million at last report. Women—such as Demi Moore, Sandra Bullock, and Julia Roberts—receive a lesser but still respectable $12.5 million a pop for their six weeks of film lensing. On TV Jerry Seinfeld pulls

1

down a reported $1 million per episode, and there are Broadway star salaries that could let you buy a nice new BMW each week if you wanted to. You want to direct? Just put it into your next contract.

Acting is also politically attractive—and politically correct—these days. The superstar is now the superartist, the superintellectual—no longer merely a rich celebrity, but spokesperson for the poor, savior of the animals, mayor of resort cities, and consort of European royalty. Superstars are no longer merely heroes to the profession; they have become role models to the public, assuming the capabilities (additional to their own) of the characters they play. Actor Jack Lemmon lectured the country on nuclear waste after performing the role of a nuclear expert in *The China Syndrome*. Actor Jack Klugman, on the basis of playing the role of a television mortician, testified before the U.S. House of Representatives on the nation's death certification policy. Actors Jane Fonda, Sissy Spacek, and Jessica Lange testified in tandem before the U.S. Senate on the subject of farm mortgage foreclosures— solely because they had played farmwomen in films; the august senators rewarded them with (what else?) a standing ovation. Indeed, Fonda—and Martin Sheen, James Edward Olmos, and Whoopie Goldberg—have on occasion taken the role of national conscience and have become role models for millions of teenagers. When the California insurance industry lost a $60 million election, its leaders decided to hire a celebrity actor "whose image will communicate integrity" to "interpret and testify on behalf of the industry on key questions and issues." An actor's image, rather than a leader's deeds, seems to be necessary to convey integrity in today's media-dominated world.

So—why not get into the act? You don't even need a college degree—or, for that matter, any previously acknowledged talent in writing papers, programming computers, or throwing the split-fingered fastball. Or even acting: heck, little children do it. Models do it. Untrained ex-athletes and ex-cons do it. Even dogs, geese, pigs, and whales do it. Let's do it: Let's act!

Hey, wait a minute! One thing that must be said before plunging in: Acting, whatever its charms, is a lousy way to make a living, by which I mean a *career* living—one that will provide you with a reasonable salary that you can count on picking up year after year and that will give you a secure base on which to buy a home, develop a long-lasting relationship, have children if you want to, and stand tall before your God, or at least your parents and siblings. An income that will allow you to consider yourself—miracle of miracles—"self-supporting."

For the number of people who actually do this—who become self-supporting through acting alone—is astonishingly small. It's probably about the same as the number who win lotteries or seats in the U.S. Senate. Yes, there are more than 100,000 professional actors in the United States. But fewer than half of them make an income higher than the national poverty level for a single person ($7,500) in any given year. And far fewer than half of *them* make that amount ten years in a row. And as far as a standard middle-class income—the salary of an average state university associate professor or librarian, for example— we would have to reckon on only 5,000 or 6,000 actors in any given year.

Putting this all together, we find that in a country with more than a million lawyers, 4.5 million mechanics, and nearly 8 million machine operators, *the number of self-supporting career actors—those who can be said to make their living as actors for at least ten years in a row—is no more than 2,000 or 3,000 people!* This is hardly a profession; it might be better described as a club. To put this in even clearer perspective: There are far more self-supporting acting *teachers* in the United States than self-supporting actors.

Let's face it squarely: Acting is one of the toughest businesses in the world to break into. Maybe *the* toughest. The majority of people who try fail even to get their foot in the door. And the vast majority of those who do get in the door don't stay there very long. It's a reality. It's raw. Hate me for saying it, but face it nonetheless. At any given time, fewer than 10% to 15% of the country's professional actors are in fact employed. The rest, obviously, are "between jobs." And for most of them, the "between" is simply a euphemism for "without."

Acting, we might say, is a boutique profession, like being a U.S. senator or a network anchorperson: Only a handful make it in. The only real problem with this situation is that acting seems to be treated (and marketed) as if it were a mass occupation. There are nearly 200 graduate actor-training programs in the nation's 1,000+ college and university theatre and drama departments, plus another 1,000 private acting schools and studios that claim to train professional actors. Just how many M.F.A. programs or private schools do you think are out there offering pre-professional training for U.S. senators or network anchorpersons? None, would be a good guess.

So there's a lot more competition than in most boutique professions. But if you've got the goods and the smarts and the opportunities and, may I say, the luck, you've got as good a crack at it as anyone. This book will give you some solid pointers.

But you're also going to have to really work at it, and that's really the most fundamental point underlying this book. Wanting it isn't enough, studying for it isn't enough, and "turning on to stardom" won't get you into the casting office. Being "discovered" at a drug store soda fountain is simply a fan magazine myth; you're going to have to work hard on your acting and work even harder on learning how to present yourself—and represent yourself—in the job market. Yes, you're going to have to market yourself. That—in the context of the "raw facts" that constitute the acting market—is what the rest of this book is about.

So, let's get started.

## THE ACTING INDUSTRY

Whatever else acting might be, it is a *job*, and a job within one of America's biggest enterprises: the entertainment industry. You should be aware of the scale of this larger world—the industry—in which an actor plies his or her craft. It's one of the biggest in the world.

Gross rental (that is, movie theatre) income from top films can now top $300 million, as 1993's *Jurassic Park*, *Forrest Gump*, and *The Lion King* all did; *E.T.* has cracked $400 million. Add in videocassette sales and licensing arrangements, and you can double the figures; *Forrest Gump* has made $650 million so far (though, by typically "creative" Hollywood accounting, it has not yet officially broken even).

Broadway shows cost up to $5 million for a play and $10 to $15 million for a musical. When they lose, they lose big: The musical *Big* lost its entire $10.3 million investment in a matter of a few weeks in 1996. But when they win . . . well, combined with their national tours, the Broadway theatre generates more than a *billion* dollars in income each year. More money is taken in annually at the Manhattan *Phantom of the Opera* box office than by the New York Yankees and Mets put together. Major regional theatres run annual budgets ranging from $5 million to $15 million. Anyone who thinks theatre is a "fabulous invalid" is looking backward through a telescope.

Entertainment these days is also a many-sided oligopoly, with vast interconnections among its many corporate members. Disney's 1995 merger with ABC, which had previously merged with Capital Cities, meant that the celebrated Mouse is now a Lion in the multiple worlds of film production (Disney, Touchstone, Miramax), television production (Buena Vista, Touchstone, DreamWorks), stage production, books, newspapers, magazines, recordings, radio, retailing, theme parks, sports teams (baseball and hockey), and sports stadia. Disney also owns a film library, nine individual TV stations, separate broadcast (ABC) and cable (Disney, ESPN, Lifetime) networks, a fleet of cruise ships, and a newly-renovated Broadway theatre on 42nd Street. Disney is even involved—at least at the development level—with productions that might be appearing in New York City (at Playwrights' Horizons, allied with DreamWorks) or at your local regional theatre. By 1997 the Disney AEA (Actor's Equity Association) contract accounted for 3.4% of all working *stage* actors' income in the United States. This is a mouse that truly roars.

But Disney is obviously not the only entertainment conglomerate. Time Warner, itself a merged corporation, merged with Turner Broadcasting (also in 1995) forming an even larger conglomerate than the Burbank Rodent: The resulting Time/Warner/Turner combo now includes—at least at the time of writing—CNN, TBS, HBO, Cinemax, Warner Brothers, Warner Books, The Cartoon Network, New Line Cinema, Castle Rock Films, *Time, Life, Sports Illustrated,* D.C. Comics, Comedy Central, and dozens of other related enterprises. TWT estimates its estimated annual earnings at 20 billion dollars, more than three times the gross domestic product of Nicaragua. Other multimedia conglomerates—such as CBS/Westinghouse, NBC/General Electric, SONY/Columbia/TriStar, Viacom/Paramount, and News Corporation/Fox—utterly dominate the industry in which actors play their professional roles. Even live stage production, long the bastion of independent individual producers like David Merrick and Alexander Cohen, has in the past twenty years become dominated by just three corporations—the Shuberts, the Nederlanders, and Jujamcyn—that own virtually all of New York's Broadway theatres and many of the touring theatres they perform in around the country. In brief: These are not the sorts of groups that hold bake sales in order to pay for the costumes.

Entertainment is not just one of the nation's largest industries; it is also one of its most economically important. American entertainment (particularly movies and television) provides the United States with—apart from airplanes—its strongest trade balance with the rest of the world: a blessing for the American economy (no matter what Bob Dole says). American films and TV shows—and the actors in them—are as familiar in Rome, Rio, Seoul, and Jakarta as they are in Peoria and Sioux Falls. Broadway musicals—many of them cast in New York—are on the boards daily in major world capitals. And the spread of American films, theatre, and TV—and of American acting—has played a major role, like it or not, in making English the world's universal entertainment language. Even foreign films these days are often filmed in English with American actors: Spain's *Things I Never Told You* was directed by Isabel Coixet in the American midwest, and *Two Much* was directed by Fernando Trueba in Miami, with Melanie Griffith. Reason: Major films need an international audience to break even. "Go above $3 million and you have to sell abroad," says a Spanish producer.

The point is, acting professionally puts you in the big leagues of a great international industry. You may rarely, if ever, see the bigwigs above—the "dreadful pudder o'er our heads," as King Lear says—but they're there, and they and their policies and influence will determine much of what goes on in your professional life. You're in business, like it or not. As Francine Witkin, a Hollywood casting director, makes clear, "Actors must understand this is a business and treat it as a business. They're a *product.* Most people don't think of themselves as products, they think of themselves as human beings with fantasies and dreams. They've got to realize what this business is and what the politics are."

## ART AND INDUSTRY

If acting is part of an industry, is it still an art?

Well, of course. Indeed, that's one of the problems of acting professionally—it's an art within an industry, within a world in which "the gross" and "B.O." are both fiscal realities and cultural metaphors.

When young actors first read a trade paper like *Variety,* they might be excused if they think they've ended up with the *Wall Street Journal* or *National Hygiene.* For "grosses" and "B.O." hold the main attention, page after page. "*Amazing Grace* grosses" headlined *Variety* when the film by that name had an "amazing gross" income at its weekend premiere. "Feminine B.O. power!" trumpeted a *Variety* column when *The First Wives Club* premiered.

Of course the gross (income) and B.O. (box office revenue) are the bottom line of the accountant's report, but grossness (in the sense of crassness) and the odor of mendacity—as Tennessee Williams might have said—often pervade the entertainment industries as well. Hollywood, of course, comes in for most of the disdain. Exposés like William Beyer's *Breaking Through, Selling Out, Dropping Dead,* Paul Sylbert's *Final Cut,* and Lynda Obst's *Hello, He Lied,* as well as plays like John Patrick Shanley's *Four Dogs and a Bone* and David Mamet's *Speed the Plow,* all show us the seamy, commercial side of tinsel town, where— we are told—lying, stealing, nepotism, lawsuits, and sexual politics are the order of the day. But the so-called "legitimate" theatre isn't all that super-legit, either. For *Speed the Plow,* the (nonprofit) Lincoln Center Theatre production company cast Madonna as the female lead—not, one must imagine, wholly for her thespian talents (though they are considerable) but for the potential contribution to the gross receipts such a sometime sex symbol and rock star might generate. The aroma of B.O. (box office, of course) knows no geography in the entertainment business.

So where do actors fit into the gross? The suits (that is, executives) are at the top, as everywhere else. As for the actors:

ESTRAGON: Where do we come in?

VLADIMIR: Come in? Come in? On our hands and knees!

(Samuel Beckett, *Waiting for Godot*)

The most fundamental law of economics, as you doubtless know, is that of supply and demand, which in part means that the more of something there is, the less anyone has to pay for it. Well, there are an awful lot of actors willing to work—a fact not lost on theatre producers. In addition to the 100,000 union actors already active in the profession, there are those 1,000+ college drama departments turning out new actors every year and an even greater number of high school drama programs, private acting schools, conservatories, and private teachers sending young men and women to New York and Hollywood with plans to "break into" the field. And there are thousands more who simply head into town on their own. The supply of actors, in other words, far exceeds the demand. And the economics reflect this.

So, while everybody in the Western world must know by now that Jim Carrey made $20 million to star in *The Cable Guy,* few realize that Carrey's fee was fully half the cost of making that film and that, consequently, the rest of the actors got a tiny fraction of that amount. In general, actor salaries below the star level are a relatively minor part of the entertainment industry budget. For all but starring actors, the union minimum pay scale—or, in Hollywood argot, "scale plus 10" (the union minimum plus 10% for your agent)—is the *maximum* pay as well. This is true for most live theatre and television, and for many films— and explains why the median actor income is well below the national poverty level, and why there are only a few hundred actors who can honestly describe themselves as self-supporting in their trade for several years in a row.

I want you to think about this. Young actors are often very idealistic about this reality of the acting business. Many are quick to point out that they don't have any desire to become "stars," but simply seek steady acting work: an acting position, say, at a modest repertory company in a medium-sized town. They will happily trade fame and riches, they say to me, for just a position with creative opportunities and artistic respectability; they don't need a lot of money, "just enough to live on." Fine. But that "just enough to live on" is the problem! Surprise, folks: Merely rejecting Broadway and Hollywood does not magically produce something in their stead, any more than rejecting an unoffered Rolls Royce will put a Hyundai in your driveway. Or even get you a driveway.

For the fact is that it is desperately difficult for a beginner to get *any* professional acting job. At any theatre. In any city. At a statistical level, your chances are about one in a hundred. One in a hundred, *literally*, and maybe even one in a thousand if the truth be known. That's the law of supply and demand working, and the supply in acting is all but unlimited. The fact is that you should no more expect to get a paid acting job on account of your B.A. in drama than you can expect to become a U.S. senator on the basis of your B.A. in political science. You can hope, of course. Expect, no.

I don't need to dwell on this any further, and I won't. Acting is still one of the most thrilling and wonderful things you can do with your life. If the raw facts don't frighten you off altogether, if you have a passion for acting and for the theatrical arts, if you think you have the gifts and the drive and emotional stability—well, then, you could surely do worse than to give it your best shot. The challenge is great, but the quest will teach you more about yourself—and more about life—than almost any other. You will find it demanding, sometimes depressing, but much of the time exhilarating as well. You're in a high stakes adventure. The rest of this book—like an adventure—might even be fun.

But always know: You're going to be in the competition of your life. Don't settle for half measures. This is—as one of my former students said—a champion business. Your competitors are every bit as dedicated as you are. They also have their dreams and their fantasies and their hometown reviews from the *Fresno Bee* and the *Keokuk Gazette*. They've read this book—or others like it—too. But realize also: They're no more likely to make it than you are—at least at this point. The path—though desperately narrow—is not altogether blocked. So go for it by all means if you want. But go for it all the way.

## DEVELOPING A MATURE VIEWPOINT

There are some hard lessons in the previous paragraphs, but they are basic adult realities, and they are lessons worth learning.

If you're going to pursue an acting career, you're going to have to deal with adult reality, and you're going to have to be an adult—while retaining enough of the childlike innocence required for any artist.

What does being an adult mean? It means, basically, that *you*—not your parents or teachers—will be taking the initiatives in your own life. You will be making (and responding to) your own assignments, as it were.

The biggest difference between life as a student and life after graduation is that after graduation nobody assigns you anything. Nobody tells you what to do next. Nobody *cares* what you do next. And there are no grades.

As wonderful as this may seem, it can lead to life's first great agonies: What do I do now? How good am I? Am I going to make it? Why doesn't anybody care about me?

Nobody in the adult world will answer those questions—unless you pay them to (in which case they are not unbiased) or unless they love you (in which case they are even more certainly not unbiased).

The rest of this book is to help you deal with these questions.

One thing to get out of your system right away, if you want to be an actor, is a desperate need for praise.

Praise is so easily given, and so inexpensive to part with, as to be functionally meaningless (and cruelly misleading) in the adult world, where it is mainly a soothing balm in the often abrasive world of doing business. It costs nothing (and therefore means nothing) for a casting director to say, "Oh, you're very talented, I love your audition!" So they say it all the time. It's simply the easiest (and safest) way to turn you down. "Hollywood is the only place where you can die of encouragement," says Pauline Kael. Nothing is more depressing than to hear actors coming back from auditions exclaiming enthusiastically, "I didn't get the part, but I feel that they *liked* me!" It's depressing because actors don't audition to be liked, but to be hired. Acting professionally is a business: What difference does it make if they like you if they never hire you? And *do* they like you? Maybe they're just trying to get rid of you. Some actors hang around for years subsisting on such dollops of empty praise.

Praise is an incentive to children. It is the A+ or the gold star or the pat on the back that induces good study habits and good behavior. But praise is mainly a lubricant in an adult business that generates enormous friction and despair among its participants. Praise is doled out by worldly-wise producers—mainly to keep you from coming back to bomb their house or kidnap their children. They may give you praise when you seem to need it, but they will give you a job only when *they* need it. And that's where you have to learn to fit in.

## HERE'S TO YOU

If you've read this far, and haven't yet thrown the book against the wall, you might just have a chance.

If you suspect that discussions of the past few pages have been designed to alarm you, your suspicions are correct.

There are much pleasanter things to say about acting as a profession, and much more positive advice to be given. The rest of the book will be in this direction.

Still, at this point, it's essential to keep before us this fact: Acting is a profession that hasn't very much room for you, and isn't going to be welcoming you to its inner sanctums. The unions, in fact, will be very actively trying to keep you out. There is hardly a producer, director, actor, or union executive who will not *routinely* advise aspiring actors not to press on. "Don't put your daughter on the stage, Mrs. Worthington, Don't put your daughter on the stage!" I have no hesitation in repeating Noel Coward's famous lyric, because the people who will press on are going to press on anyway. And they're probably among the few who are going to make it, too.

# Chapter 2

# What You Will Need

If you are going to make it—that is, if you are going to make a livelihood as an actor—then you must possess the following:

- Talent
- A charming / fascinating / interesting / likable / hateful definable *personality*
- Looks, and certain physical characteristics
- Training
- Experience
- Contacts
- Commitment and a massive will to succeed
- A healthy attitude and a capacity for psychological adjustment
- Freedom from entanglements and inhibitions
- Good information, advice, and help
- Luck

You might want to rebel at some of these items, such as "contacts," "looks," or "freedom from inhibitions." But these requirements should not be understood in a negative sense. You do not have to be the son of a film editor, or a Miss Georgia contestant, to succeed as an actor—and you certainly do not have to sleep with the casting director. Developing contacts, becoming flexible in your acting, and caring for your personal health, however, are extremely important to career success. Each of the requirements listed is a basic ingredient for professional work, and each deserves a full discussion.

## TALENT

I'm afraid the first requirement for success still is acting talent. It is of far greater importance than any other factor. Talent is the *sine qua non* of a performer, and while there are certainly those who make a brief professional appearance without it, lasting success comes only to those who have it.

But what the hell *is* it? And do *you* have it? Well, these are questions on which neuroses are based.

"Talent: I can't define it, but I know it when I see it." Almost everyone says this, one way or another, and it makes perfectly good sense. Talent is essentially a kind of *communication*. And since it is mostly non-verbal, it is not defined so much as it is recognized. "Magnetism," "electricity," stage "presence"—these are the metaphors we use to discuss talent, describing those qualities that make a person communicate (project) a compelling personality, without simply pushing themselves on us.

Talent is a *two-way exchange* with the audience. It's not simply something you have within you, but it's also your ability to interact with an audience. To share—give and take—with an audience. We, the audience, will define your talent as much as you, the actor, will reveal it.

Personal magnetism or "electricity" (think of it as "alternating current") is the ability to draw others to you, to inspire them, to lead them with your words, your body, and your eyes. It is the ability to establish rapport and set up mutual vibrations, both intellectually and emotionally. It is the ability to enter into mutual feedback with other actors, and with an audience as well.

*Confidence* is central to talent; some say talent is *only* that. Confidence is the power you have over your own personality; it allows you to be unafraid in your own persona, to stand tall and easy on your own feet, to accept criticism freely—and at the same time to rise above it. *You* have to develop this confidence too, of course. Think of it as a test of your talent, rather than as a subservience to your critics.

Talent allows you to *believe* in yourself: in the reality of your performance and in the reality of your "being an actor"—even when no one else does. You may have substantial doubts about your potential for long-term career success, but you can never doubt that you "are" an actor. That is a belief that must be in your bones, sustaining itself through every interview and every audition, so that it shows even though you make no *effort* to show it. This belief is your authority; it gives you the power that allows you to galvanize every aspect of personality and every bit of training and experience into an exciting and apparently artless performance or audition.

Do you have talent? How do you tell? You can't rely on mere compliments, good grades, or the old devil word: praise. Rather note this: As a performer, you should be *getting cast*. In college or in neighborhood plays, you should be auditioning for—*and getting*—major roles, or at least you should be regularly considered for them. If, after two or three years of training as an actor, you are still unsuccessful at getting major roles in college or community theatre productions, and if they're going to people you think are less than terrific (and, of course, if your casting is not being hampered by political considerations beyond your control), you should begin to reconsider your career goals. Tough advice, but better now than later. "Major" roles, of course, are not defined just by size; they are the roles you *want* to play, the roles you think you *ought* to play. While it may be perfectly true that "there are no small roles, only small actors," the fact remains that only a major role will fully expand and test your abilities. The size of a role is not always of primary consequence; the depth, breadth, wit, passion, individuality, and "electricity" of the role are the characteristics that determine whether it provides this sort of talent test.

In general, the people who rise to successful careers and even stardom are recognized as very talented from the very beginning. Craft and experience can be acquired along the way, but talent, where it exists, shows up almost immediately.

On the other hand, extraordinary talent does not mean perfection of performance or anything close to it. Extraordinarily talented people have been known to sink in one disaster after another. They perform badly, they cannot be heard, they aren't believable, they do the same thing over and over, they get too fat or too thin, they're always committing some terrible error or other, and they frequently reap the derision of their peers, teachers, and even their directors. I remember four actors at the Yale Drama School when I was there in the mid-1960s who were always being criticized by their fellow students. Even their teachers regularly despaired of their "bad habits" and frequent "lapses." Their names were Stacy Keach, Sam Waterston, Daniel Travanti, and Joan Van Ark. All, of course, have had brilliant careers on the stage and screen. And we all knew that would happen. Why? Because come audition time, the four of them were *always cast*. Directors (like myself) fought like wildcats over them. The proof is in the putting—of names on cast lists.*

Talent means all that we have discussed, and more still. It *can* mean, in addition:

- That a person sings, dances, juggles, tells jokes, walks tightropes, or does striptease, backflips, handsprings, or T'ai Chi. Most talented people can do some of these; many more think they are talented because they can do one or two. A person who is genuinely talented need not be able to sing on key, but can probably "sell" a song if called upon to do so. The more skills a person has, obviously, the more employable he or she is.

- That a person can communicate nuances clearly yet subtly. That an actor can vary inflection and timing so as to communicate what a director wants, without excessive coaching or reworking. Whether the actor does this by technique or instinct is not the concern of this book, but that the actor must be *able* to do it, and do it rapidly, particularly during an audition, everyone agrees.

- That a person has a flexible, mobile, and expressive voice and body. These are the actor's basic tools. At the outset, the actor must be in possession of an expressive speaking voice—one that communicates what is between the lines , one that connotes something beyond the mere words spoken. Similarly, the talented person communicates in body movement and repose, naturally assumes interesting positions and postures, and is—yes—attractive to look at. Sex appeal is obviously related to this, and although that is not by a long shot the whole story, it is clear that an audience sensually intrigued is an audience already on its way to admiring and relishing a performance. Casting directors have never been oblivious to this, and you shouldn't be either.

- That a person is relaxed in front of others, and when performing for others, and *enjoys* performing. This enjoyment is said to result from an exhibitionistic instinct, and nothing in my experience contradicts that. Though actors may be as shy as anyone else (and not a few of them are painfully shy), some part of their personality

---

*Brief cavil: This isn't *always* true, of course. Nobody starts out, even in school, getting cast all the time—or even some of the time. Kevin Costner couldn't even get cast in his state college production of *Rumpelstiltskin*. Out of twenty-five Dartmouth students auditioning for a 1957 production of *Macbeth*, twenty-three were cast in the play; the two leftovers were myself and Marc Austin. (Happy ending: We both went on to become professional actors. Maybe that's why I'm writing this book.)

relishes contact with others, even via the formal medium of theatre or film.

These are all aspects of "talent," and the word is often used to denote one or more of them. There are no firm prerequisites for "making it" in show business, but the necessity for talent comes as close as any possibly could.

## PERSONALITY

Personality is the second most important characteristic of the successful actor, a ranking that often draws shrieks of dismay. "What does my personality have to do with it? Use me for my talent and ability. My personality is my own business!" Sorry, but no. As the American actor William Gillette said more than three generations ago,

> Among those elements of Life and Vitality, but greatly surpassing all others in importance, is the human characteristic or essential quality which passes under the execrated name of Personality. The very word must send an unpleasant shudder through this highly sensitive Assembly; for it is supposed to be quite the proper and highly cultured thing to sneer at Personality as an altogether cheap affair and not worthy to be associated for a moment with what is highest in Dramatic Art. Nevertheless, cheap or otherwise, inartistic or otherwise, and whatever it really is or not, it is the most singularly important factor for infusing the Life-Illusion into modern stage creations that is known to man.

The passage of eighty years has not changed the import of Mr. Gillette's well-capitalized observations; if anything, it has emphasized them further. American theatre performances have been dominated, at least since World War II, by the Konstantin Stanislavsky/Lee Strasberg "Method" school of acting, which emphasizes the actor's personal (or "real life") truthfulness—and therefore the actor's own personality —within the fiction of the role. And the revolution toward *cinema vérité,* or "truthful filmmaking," brought the Method—or something like it— to mid-century moviemaking as well, and made the personality o movie actors central to whatever character they played. Actors whe can, in Stanislavsky's famous expression "live the life of their characte: on stage," are now most likely to live it in the casting office and audi tion room as well. Which means they live it in daily life. Which means it *is* their life: It's their day-to-day personality.

This is particularly true of film and television acting (not to mention in "real TV"), where the snappy production schedule virtually requires instant characterization and immediate performance. There is precious little rehearsal in commercial films or television. "More often than not, you arrive and you're expected to start acting immediately," says John Lithgow, the Broadway and film actor also starring in *Third Rock from the Sun.* "The director hardly has a word to say to you. You'd be amazed. You arrive, the camera rolls, and you start acting." Natasha McElhone, who played Francoise Gilot in the film *Surviving Picasso,* reports she never had a chance even to discuss what her relationship with her Picasso, co-star Anthony Hopkins, might be. "We just did it," she says. "We met, effectively, on day one, when we shot the scene where I'm running down the road. . . . We have a big row, and he's shaking me, and it ends up with his tongue down my throat. That was literally the first thing that the two of us had to do with one another." If you are a day player on television—someone hired to do a small part with lines that can be filmed on a single day—you can be cast the day before, get your script that evening, arrive on the set at 8:00 the next morning with your lines learned, be shooting by 10:00, and have your work completed before lunch. Your "personality" is your character; it's as simple as that, since there's no time for anything else. Bill Cosby yells at you, you shriek, and suddenly you're "Linda, the delivery woman" shrieking instead of "Robyn, the actress" shrieking. And that's why your personality is crucial—because at the audition you shrieked like they saw Linda shrieking, and now you're Linda (the director may not even know your real name) because you seem to have what they think is a "Linda personality," which is why you were hired: because they didn't want to take the time to teach it to you (and they probably didn't know what it was until they saw it).

Casting people, particularly in Hollywood, live by this policy daily, of course. For film and television, 90% of the major casting decisions for feature roles—among the agent-submitted professional actors with roughly equal credits—is made at the interview stage: which means, therefore, on the basis of your looks and your personality—what Hollywood people generally call your "quality"—not your talent. A typical call might bring in fifty actors for an interview, and call back only five of them to actually audition. This means, of course, that *90% of the professional actors submitted by agents for the job are rejected*—without even showing what they can "do" with the part. "Quality," and not imagination or craft, provides the big first sift.

And while auditions remain *de rigeur* in the legitimate stage—and interviews rarely take place apart from them—the importance of a stageworthy personality—one suited to the role, that is—is still enormously important in live theatre as well. For while the legitimate theatre remains a medium where characterization can be created through the rehearsal process, that rehearsal process may be a lot shorter than yours was in college; and time—which is expensive in the professional world—is much more at a premium. American stage directors, often working somewhat improvisationally, may seek to employ your personal characteristics and idiosyncrasies as much as possible, gaining thereby an individuality in your part otherwise unavailable. All this demands that a great portion of "the real you"—your own personality—be employed in the service of the performance.

Yet it is not sufficient merely to have a personality that is "right for the role." You must also have, or seem to have, a widely *appealing* or *exciting* personality. "Likability" is the crucial factor in acting, says professional actor manager Bud Robinson, and audience appeal (and audience excitement) translate readily into the fiscal bottom line. In Hollywood, a numerical personality rating system, known as TVQ, is often used in casting decisions, and actors are awarded "Q scores" on the basis of what audiences think of them, *as people*. Politically active performers, such as Jane Fonda and Ed Asner (who calls TVQ "McCarthyism"), have been hurt in the Q ratings, despite their unquestioned acting skills; less controversial actors have scored higher. "A low Q score could spell disaster," says the Screen Actors Guild, in lamenting the TVQ's attempt to put a dollar value on an actor's perceived personality.

What is a good acting personality? It is no one thing in particular, but it is definable in general terms. You are shy, you are fascinating, you are profound, you are dangerous, you are aggressive, you are hostile, you are nasty, you are fiery, you are sensual, you are youthful, you are idealistic, you are wacky, you are serene.

A warning: That you are *nice* will get you nowhere. Nice isn't a personality. Thousands of aspiring actors have failed in interviews simply by being nice, polite, and forgotten. What's wrong with nice? It's proper enough, but it's also dull, it's unexciting, and it doesn't bring people into the theatres. Yes, I'm afraid, there *is* an "interview technique," and you will have to learn it (some tips are given in the following section). A hundred actors will grouse, "I didn't get the job because I don't play their games at the interview. I'm just not that kind of person." But it's not a game, and you *must become* that kind of person. Interview technique is nothing but letting other people see just what kind of person you are—*when you're not in an interview*. The trick is that you have to show this *in* an interview. This may in fact be the truest test of your acting! If your day-to-day personality is hidden in your interview behind a dozen "pleased-to-meet-yous" and a score of "thank-you-very-muches," you will never be looked at further. When you retreat into timid subservience at an interview, you not only fail to "play the interview game," you insist on playing another game: the "good little girl" or "good little boy" game that got you so far in the principal's office. Well, perhaps for the first time in your life, this is the wrong game to play.

Successful actors are not bland people. That is not to say that they are wantonly brash or abrasive. Most actors of my acquaintance are people with depth, sensitivity, dedication, and artistry. Their personalities are not applied for the sake of calling attention to themselves. The surest way to lose your personality is to spin out a fake one. Your real personality will follow you in every role you play; it will become your trademark. In the classic days of Hollywood, such trademarks were Bogart's toughness, John Wayne's reckless virility, Fonda's sensitive passion, Marilyn Monroe's soft, defenseless sexuality, Marlon Brando's vulnerable egotism, W.C. Fields's cynicism, Mae West's leering defiance, Grace Kelly's poise, and Clark Gable's cockiness. These were not "put on" personalities; they were intrinsic to their owners and vital to their owners' successes. The personalities of today's rising stars are more subtle, perhaps, but just as ingrained in their performances, even in varied characterizations.

You cannot create your personality—your stage personality—but you can liberate it. What are your personal characteristics? What do others see in you? Find out and let those characteristics come out. Do not worry about "your good features versus your bad features." Just have features. Don't be afraid to be different. Don't opt for the ordinary, for the timid, for the nice. Don't try to be what you think they want you to be. Don't worry about yourself. Be proud of yourself. *Like yourself.* If you don't, it's hard to see how somebody else will.

One other aspect of personality deserves some attention, one so obvious that most young actors completely ignore it: Does the director enjoy talking with you? There should be nothing surprising about this. Like everyone else, directors want to enjoy their work, and they would rather work with people they like than with people they don't like. Just as you do. There is an artistic component to this principle as well. Filmmaker William Bayer advises would-be directors, "In the end the most important quality to look for in an actor may be rapport: Are you going to be able to work with this actor on a basis of intimate friendship? When a film is shooting and the pressure is on, friendship and understanding may be the qualities that have most to do with failure or success." While there is no assured way of generating that rapport, you should be able to recognize its importance, and open yourself up to it without feeling guilty. Perhaps it is safe to say that if you are the kind of person who combines vivacity with sensitivity, and sincerity with charm, then you might be the kind of person a director would choose for company—and for the Company.

## LOOKS AND PHYSICAL "TYPE"

Acting is one of the only professions (modeling is another) where looks count *openly* and *legally*. Looks probably count in other professions as well, but nobody talks about it, and I suppose I shouldn't either.

But in acting your physical "type" (fat and jolly, lean and hungry, nerdish and owly, for example) will normally play a crucial role in the role you get to play—or even get to audition for. There are times—particularly in roles that have no speaking lines—that you can be hired on the basis of your looks alone.

And you can get *rejected* on those same grounds, of course: if, for example, you are too old, too young, too fat, too short, too "ethnic"—or not ethnic enough—in the eyes of the producer or director. Or, in those same eyes, if you are a member of the wrong sex, or the wrong race, or are differently abled than other folks who happen to be available.

Indeed, the acting business is just about the world's last remaining *un*equal opportunity employer. And this is all—so far, anyway—perfectly legal. For casting inequalities are endemic to acting. This is not necessarily a matter of simple prejudice or mean-spiritedness, I hasten to say: An actor is hired not merely to perform a role, but to *depict* a specific character, whose race and sex and general appearance may be deemed—by the author, director, producer, and/or even by you, the actor—absolutely necessary to the play's or film's meaning and impact (not to mention its box office appeal). It is certainly understandable that Martin Scorcese, for example, cast Robert DeNiro rather than—to take some extreme examples—Cecily Tyson or Woody Allen in the role of Jake LaMotta in *Raging Bull;* LaMotta was a real-world American boxing champion, still well-remembered by many in the film's intended audience, and the film was basically naturalistic, so it is hardly an insult to Tyson's or Allen's acting abilities to say that their "type" precluded their being cast in this role. Indeed, DeNiro himself felt he had to gain fifty pounds to play it.

Much of this is changing, however, and changing rapidly. Women's role potential has certainly been on the increase in recent years; at time of writing, women garner 36% of principal TV and film roles, up 50% from when the first edition of this book was written twenty-five years ago. Nor are these roles relegated to homemaker and servant: Women play 16% of the roles with presumed advanced degrees— almost three times more than in the 1960s. Thus *Variety*, the major international newspaper of show business, trumpeted that 1996 was "The Year of the Woman—FOR REAL." The same is true on stage, with a vast increase over the past decade in women playwrights, artistic directors, play directors, and actors. There are also more plays, movies, and television shows about women than there used to be, by a large margin, and a significant number of male characters played by women on the world's stages. Two internationally celebrated productions of *King Lear* in the mid-90s, for example, one in New York and the other in Berlin, featured actresses in the title role. Female Hamlets, Malvolios, Richards the Second, and Oberons are increasingly seen on stages professional and amateur. Gender-bending the other way happens as well: A six-foot, two-hundred pound *man* played the bad little girl in *The Bad Seed* to great acclaim in a 1996 production in Los Angeles. Many important recent plays, such as Caryl Churchill's *Cloud Nine* and Tony Kushner's *Angels in America,* play virtual hash with gender, double-casting men and women as women and men with virtual abandon. Film casting is more and more genderblind—or gender-irrelevant —as well. Women have played male roles—in one case, Linda Hunt played Billy Kwan in *The Year of Living Dangerously,* winning an Oscar in the process—and increasingly women play, as women, roles that used to be exclusively male. The celebrated Goldie Hawn line in *The First Wives Club* (itself a breakthrough film for female actors), "There are only three roles for women now: babe, D.A., and *Driving Miss Daisy,*" only emphasizes the increasing percentage of female district attorneys who appear in contemporary cinema—as well as female judges, lawyers, surgeons, psychiatrists, CEOs, soldiers, detectives (who can forget Frances McDormand in *Fargo?*), and combat pilots (or Meg Ryan in *Courage Under Fire?*)—in addition to the Daisys and the babes. When the last edition of this book came out, the feminization of these previously "male type" roles was still in process: The parts played by Sigourney Weaver in *Alien,* Debra Winger in *Legal Eagles,* and Whoopie Goldberg in *Burglar* had been initially written for men but were won in the casting office by those talented women. Today, the roles probably would have been written female, or at least gender-neutral, to begin with. And why not? Females now occupy the CEO roles of production studios as well, with Sherry Lansing as president of Paramount Pictures and Jamie Tarses as president of ABC Entertainment as we go to press.

And colorblind casting—casting without regard to race—is equally ubiquitous in both theatre and film. Certainly, African-American actors are relatively mainstreamed now, to the extent that they are represented in American films and television commercials at approximately the same level (roughly 12%) as they are in the U.S. population overall —up from a shocking 0.5% thirty years ago. And they often represent an even higher percentage of actors performing on Broadway: Since the late 90s black actors have, on various weeks in the season, represented 25% to 30% of the performers on New York's celebrated "Great White Way." Nor are African-American actors, despite what many think, particularly typed into criminal roles; they represent barely 8% of the crooks on prime-time TV, where whites commit crimes against blacks twice as frequently as the other way around. Overall, blacks are more likely to appear on TV in business, managerial, and professional occupations than as blue collar, clerical, or unemployed.

It would be folly, though, to think that race and gender have become immaterial in the casting process. They have not, and most likely will not.

Hispanics remain poorly represented in the acting business. Although they account for 9% of Americans, they represent only 3.5% of the principal actors in film and TV, and probably fewer on the stage. Moreover, they are often relegated to roles within a "narrow spectrum from villains to second bananas," according to a recent study. Asians and Native Americans are also cast in much lower proportion to their percentage of our population in virtually all media.

Age discrimination for both sexes is also often alleged, particularly in films and TV, given the youth-oriented demographics facing TV advertisers and movie theatre exhibitors. Despite the occasional *Daisy,* or *Grumpy Old Men,* there are probably more under-twenties on TV these days than over-fifties, and "the outlook for senior actors in Hollywood remains surprisingly glum," reports *Back Stage West* magazine, citing, for example, Christopher Noth's replacement, at the hoary age of thirty-eight, by Benjamin Bratt, thirty, in *Law and Order,* "in order to give the show a younger 'Generation X' voice." Such news might not immediately threaten most of the readers of this book, but it should cause a certain anxiety for anyone contemplating a long-term career in this field.

And, despite their gains, women actors remain vastly underrepresented, both in numbers and in influence. Thirty-six percent may be half again higher than it was twenty-five years ago, but it's half again *under* the percentage of women in American life. Women between "D.A. and Miss Daisy"—that is, between forty and sixty, which can be prime ages for male actors—seem rare on stage, often nonexistent in film: "At forty, women seem to drop off the face of the earth," says a SAG spokesperson. Women's roles remain woefully limited in some quarters: Award-winning actress Joan Allen complains that most of her roles are now "the mom who sends her kids off on an adventure and watches with hands clasped for them to come home safely. She's on the first two pages and the last two pages of the script." Women's earnings —particularly at the top—are far less than their counterparts. While fifteen males made *Fortune* magazine's list of top-salaried actors in 1995–1996, only two females (Roseanne and Sandra Bullock) did.

And colorblind, genderblind casting may have leveled off, or even peaked. After twenty years of "alternative" and "gender-bender" casting, the vast majority of Romeos are still male, Juliets female, and Henry V's Caucasian. And there is increasing opposition to colorblindness in the casting business these days from a variety of quarters. Robert Brustein, artistic director of the American Repertory Theatre, has complained that "Funding agencies have started substituting sociological criteria for aesthetic criteria." The great African-American playwright August Wilson, though passionately opposing Brustein's view, still agrees—from an entirely different perspective—that "colorblind casting is an aberrant idea that has never had any validity other than as a tool of the Cultural Imperialists. . . ." Wilson's view is that colorblind casting obscures the reality of race in the effort to create homogenized drama and stifle a vigorous black theatre, arguing that "to mount an all-black production of *Death of a Salesman* or any other play conceived for white actors as an investigation of the human condition through the specifics of white culture is to deny us our own humanity, or own history, and the need to make our own investigations from the cultural ground on which we stand as black Americans. It is an assault on our presence, our difficult but honorable history in America; it is an insult to our intelligence, our playwrights, and our many and varied contributions to the society and the world at large." Obviously, the issues involved in "blind" casting—which are ethical as well as professional and social—are not going to be easy to resolve to everyone's satisfaction.

Of course, your physical type is not a matter of gender and race alone. Whether you have standard or nonstandard abilities—whether or not you are differently-abled—is also a factor in casting. Indeed, to be differently-abled may be a factor in your favor. The Hollywood-based *Players Directory*, about which more later, allows you to call attention to those specific disability categories into which you might fall, including having a visual, hearing, or walking impairment, being an arm or leg amputee, or being developmentally disabled. Howie Seago, a deaf actor, starred in Peter Sellar's staging of *The Persians* at the Mark

Taper Forum in Los Angeles, and in *Star Trek: The Next Generation.* "I have made the work myself by my own perseverance," Seago reports. He actually proposed the deaf character on *Star Trek* to the producers himself, and they bought the idea.

Julyana Soelistyo, a 4' 10" Indonesian actor, has turned her size and high-pitched voice into a casting plus: She got rave reviews from the *New York Times* and the Associated Press for her performance as Eng Ahn in David Henry Hwang's *Golden Child,* playing both an 87-year-old woman and a 10-year-old girl. "I'm very small," Soelistyo says, "so I've used it to my advantage." Barbara Adside, who is legless, has performed on dozens of TV shows over the years. "They gave me every excuse in the book—from insurance to what-not—for why I would not be able to take acting classes or be on stage for theatrical productions," Adside says, adding that directors and producers "usually have a pre-conceived notion that somebody with a disability will slow down production." But Adside does everything, with or without prosthetic legs: It can be done.

Some of your physical characteristics, however, are more variable than sex, race, and physical handicap. Your weight, dress, health, posture, hair style, teeth, complexion, and grooming all allow you great latitude. How can an actor use these variables?

As with personality, there is no classic norm.

As with personality, the premium is on a specific, *memorable* and *definable* "look," and that look should be within a specific time-honored "type."

Types exist, and they exist today exactly as they did a hundred years ago: male and female "children," "younger leading men," "ingenues," "leading men," "leading women," "character men and comedians," and "character women and comediennes." There are subgroups, but these eight remain the basic ones. The *Players Directory,* which is a publication of photographs of all working actors in the Los Angeles area, and an invaluable tool in the casting process, divides actors into these categories for the convenience of producers. So does the *Players Guide,* a comparable publication in New York. In both books,* if you aren't listed in the right category, you won't even be looked at.

> "Children" designates actors 12 years old and younger. "Preteens" are those from 13 to 15, and "teens" from 16 to 19. Ordinarily these character types are not involved in romantic affairs. On stage, anyway.

---

*The *Players Guide* was temporarily discontinued in late 1996, but it is scheduled to reappear in the stands in fall of 1997.

"Ingenues" (girls) and "young leading men" are in the "first love" category. Usually they are in the early to mid-twenties and send off vibrations of youth, innocence, and charm.

"Leading men" and "leading ladies" are, by contrast, wiser, more experienced lovers; glamorous, romantic, mature, sophisticated, in their mid-twenties to mid-forties and beyond.

"Character men," "character women," "comedians," and "comediennes" are not romantic in a conventional sense. They are usually older, and their appearance is likely to be distinctive rather than attractive.

Notice that types are not defined solely by age, but also by a position on some sort of romantic/sexual scale. This is simply an accurate reading of the typing that is done in theatre and film casting. No one assumes that an unattractive character cannot be portrayed in a romantic role (as in Stephen Sondheim's *Passion*). It is just that to do so is to cast deliberately against type, and such casting is done rarely except when a specific play or film calls for it. Since the time of Aristophanes, audiences have expected ingenues to be young and innocent, lovers to be beautiful and sensitive, and comics to be old and pudgy. Few casting directors wish to disappoint an audience.

It is important to find your type, if only to get yourself in the right chapter of the *Players Directory* or the *Players Guide*. More than that, your type will categorize you in the producer's mind. You are provided with a convenient label—a basis for comparison with other actors. You protest: You are an individual, not a type! Well, if you are Demi Moore, you don't need a label. If you aren't, you have to start somewhere. Even "male" or "female" is a label, and you can be at least a little more specific than that.

You must decide whether you can play juveniles, for example. Either you can play 14-year-olds or you cannot. Perhaps you can do a passable job, of course, but can you do better than a *real* 14-year-old? If so, sign up, because producers hate to use real 14-year-olds if they can avoid it. (Hollywood studios really hate to use any performers younger than 18, because they can only work them for limited hours; also the studio must pay to have a tutor on the set. If you are 19 and can play 12, they will love you.)

And if you are going for romantic leads, particularly in film or television, you had better be very attractive. Indeed, *very* attractive. This may sound a bit unsettling, but it's simply a fact: Casting calls openly call for "gorgeous" or "beautiful" women—sometimes they even stipulate, quite shamelessly, "staggeringly beautiful." And the quest for male "hunks" whose very entrance will send the (largely female) soap opera audiences into a rapturous fantasy animates most daytime television casting directors.

Please don't underestimate the lengths to which TV and film casting directors will try to hunt out *extraordinarily* beautiful people, too. They are not just looking for collegiate charm and boyish/girlish attractiveness; they are seeking real knock-out sex appeal, an appeal that will make viewers leave one soap for another. A 1% change in the ratings can mean millions of dollars—not for you, but for somebody— and if a sexier smile or a bouncier bosom will generate that extra percent, that's where the casting will go. This doesn't get talked about much, but it's real. That's why you'll find all the ads in the trade papers for dentists and plastic surgeons. Tooth capping, porcelain laminate veneers, nose jobs, breast implants and reductions, chin tucks, and face lifts—all of these are commonly known in the world of actors. Mariel Hemingway's silicone implants, in conjunction with her role as a *Playboy* centerfold even made national newswires. It is beyond the scope of this book to make surgical suggestions, but if you are planning to be up for straight romantic roles, you should at least take a close look at your teeth, and get some specialists to work with you on your hair and (for women, anyway) makeup.

You should clearly be a character actor or not. Weight and age have a lot to do with this: Character actors since Roman times have invariably been fat or old, if not fat *and* old, if not fat and old and *ugly*. You should surely know if you're fat or not, and you should be either fat or not fat—nothing in-between. Don't be neither fish nor fowl here. If you are ten or twenty pounds overweight, you are dead in the water. Either get your weight down to where it should be (and a bit lower in TV, since the tube will round you out a little) or gain forty more. And if you feel you are ugly, don't worry about trying to hide it. *Cultivate* it. Make it work for you. Use what you have to create a distinctive appearance. There is no "bad" appearance except a bland, characterless, typeless one.

What should you look like? That's your choice. Classic good looks, out for a while, are back in. Demi Moore and Hugh Grant could have made it in the 50s as easily as the 90s. Certain "nonclassic" looks "come in" from time to time: urban ethnic (Dustin Hoffman, John Malkovich, Al Pacino, Richard Dreyfuss, Wesley Snipes, Antonio Banderas) has been a particularly dominant look for leading men in recent years, while down-to-earth frankness (Meryl Streep, Sigourney Weaver, Whoopi Goldberg, Holly Hunter, Sandra Bullock) seems to have largely replaced the bosomy voluptuousness that characterized most leading women of the past. All these "looks" can be cultivated, and in fact *have* been cultivated by most if not all of the actors who exhibit them.

The specifics of personal physical appearance are not individually important. What counts is the effect that your person and your "image" create, and the power of that effect, which should be enormous. If you are a leading man, you must appeal to women; if a woman, you must appeal to men. There are all kinds of ways of doing that, and for some it comes more naturally than for others. But you *can* do it if you're willing to devote some time, a little money, and a frankly self-critical attitude to the matter. The main difference between professional and amateur theatre auditions is the relative lack of concern most amateurs have over their personal appearance. Actually, this is a subtle form of arrogance: Let the Star of Bethlehem arise to shine over my hidden virtue. The folly of this proto-Messianic approach need not be discussed further.

Cultivate a *distinctive* appearance. Separate yourself from the rest of your friends. Find an exciting hairstyle for yourself, a natural one perhaps, but one that looks better on you than on anybody else, one that is not seen around too much. Dress distinctively. If you are a woman and you like going around in pinpoint shirts and slim leather coats, then get some that fit right, and some great accessories, and look terrific. The perfect jacket or sweater or slacks can make a nondescript male very descript indeed. They've got to remember you *somehow* when you leave the room—and they've got to remember your individual qualities. Extravagance and propriety are not worth a dram in this business, but distinction *in your own terms* is. Find yourself, and find in yourself a unique appearance that will intrigue others.

How about your weight? Unless you're bound and determined to be a character actor, get it down. And get your physical condition up to par—and better than par. Work out regularly. Most Americans are a bit overweight and a bit unfit, but most performers aren't, as most roles aren't written for chubby, flaccid actors. This is no accident. Characters in plays and films serve as role models to the public, and role models these days tend toward the lissome, lithe, strong, and supple. The physical demands of performing also reward those who are physically capable of meeting them, so exercise, diet, and get in *great* shape. This is particularly true if you have plans toward film and television, where the camera adds ten or fifteen pounds to you anyway. For young actors, heavy character roles are few. Take a look at the young people playing the three-line parts on television programs. These are the parts you will be going for if you're just starting out, and chances are they aren't heavyweights on the scales.

How do you *use* your appearance? It precedes you in every interview and every audition. No actor can begin to look for work without a set of photographs. They are your letters of introduction. (See the section on photographs in the next chapter. You may want to read it in conjunction with this one.) Your photographs must show just what your appearance must show: originality, vitality, distinctiveness. If you look like something out of a high school yearbook, the chances are that you will never be heard of again. And if you *are* like something out a high school yearbook, the same ignominy will result!

## TRAINING AND EXPERIENCE

*Every* actor must have training and experience. No matter how naturally talented, attractive, sexy, and individual you are, you will flop in the audition if you don't know what to do. In the old days, actors without formal training were the rule. As Hermione Gingold once said, "I got all the schooling any actress needs. That is, I learned to write enough to sign contracts." John Wayne bragged that he just learned his lines and went out and said them. Now, this sort of attitude has become very definitely the exception. Training in the art and craft of acting is a virtual necessity for a successful career, and if you *are* hired at first without training, as child actors or retired athletes often are in TV, you will need it before going much further.

What sort of training should you take? A virtual explosion over the past two decades in the area of arts education has spawned an extraordinary proliferation of drama schools and actor-training institutes, and the aspiring actor has many options.

### University Training

A general college education, perhaps with a drama or theatre major, followed by a Master of Fine Arts degree from a qualified institute of higher learning, has clearly become the most desirable training base for professional *stage* actors, some of whom go on to become film/TV actors as well.

Stage acting, which remains based to a certain extent on the performer's sensitivity to literary values, acquaintanceship with political and social history, understanding of philosophical dichotomies, and general appreciation of art and culture, is favorably developed in an environment where classical as well as modern works are regularly analyzed, criticized, and performed. With nearly 200 university drama departments now offering graduate acting degrees, the opportunity to receive advanced training, usually from instructors who have professional backgrounds and ongoing contacts, is available throughout the country. While it remains true, in the classic expression of the late Joseph Papp, that "a Ph.D. won't get you through the turnstile of the IRT (the New York subway)," a strong college degree followed by advanced university actor training can give you that important entree to regional theatre stage work, and help you get from there to other media. "We are hard pressed even to *look* at someone without an Equity card or an M.F.A.," says Lee Shallat, former casting director for the South Coast Repertory Theatre, "and most of the other LORT (League of Resident Theatres) companies feel the same way."

First-class Bachelor of Fine Arts (B.F.A.) degree programs can provide a firm training foundation for a professional acting career as well. The B.F.A. should not be confused with the B.A.: It's sort of an M.F.A. at the undergraduate level; all you need—besides loads of talent—is a high school diploma to get in. The best B.F.A. programs can be every bit as focused, demanding, and intense as their masterly equivalents. They also have the benefit of getting you out in the field two or three years earlier. Of course, you won't be taking all those Medieval English and Physics for Nonmajors courses, so you (and your parents) will have to decide if this is a proper educational track for you: It also means putting almost all your academic eggs in the acting basket, of course, which doesn't give you a lot of fall-back options if the jobs don't come your way after graduation.

The best college theatre departments provide preparation for more than just stage acting. Most good departments also offer opportunities in acting for the camera as well. Even if they don't, university stage training has become increasingly important in film and TV casting worlds. "I love stage-trained actors; they are believable, they are funny, they know what to do," says Jeff Greenberg, casting director for *Frasier* and *Wings*. "I think theatre people are just fantastic," concurs Lucy Grimes, casting director for daily television (*The Young and Restless*). "The minute I see that they have some theatre training or I see them in a little theatre production, I try to use them," she continues. Susan Bedsow, executive producer of *One Life to Live* (and a former Broadway actress), tells me that she and her casting colleagues prefer to cast college-trained actors, and specifically *classically* trained actors, in soap operas because such actors are more readily able to create an "ongoing character in depth."

Nicholas Walker, cast right out of college as a daytime TV regular, had "trained" mainly by playing the title roles in college productions of *Hamlet, Richard III,* and *Peer Gynt;* he had never so much as taken an acting-for-the-camera course. Many film actors got their start in the summer Shakespeare circuit: Michael Moriarty was at the Colorado Shakespeare Festival, Stacy Keach at the Oregon Shakespeare Festival, and Tom Hanks at the Great Lakes Shakespeare Festival before they turned to cinema. David Schwimmer, graduate of Northwestern University's theatre program and star of the NBC series *Friends,* writes that his college training "made me realize that acting is a craft. With training, you can play various roles from different periods and styles of theatre. Doing a Joe Orton black comedy is very different from doing a Neil Simon play, which is very different from doing Noel Coward. All three are comedies, but very different in style, presentation, and technique. You don't have a lot of opportunity in the film industry to apply those techniques because, mostly, when you walk into a casting office they expect you to be the guy or be the girl, but I think the actors that have the most longevity in their careers are those who can transform themselves into playing beyond just who they are. Northwestern arms you for that." University drama training is becoming more and more the rule in all acting media. Actors who may previously have hid their university credentials behind a rock and pretended that Shakespeare was a Houston shortstop now brag about their academic and classical credits in their "Who's in the Cast" program write-ups and in their capsule biographies in popular magazines.

The "academicization" of the acting arts is a relatively new phenomenon. Much of it has been connected with the great growth in nonprofit legitimate theatre. Today there are over 200 such theatres, while only about a dozen existed before 1960. Nonprofit theatres often have academic roots; many if not most of them were formed by the faculties of, or graduates from, strong M.F.A. or B.F.A. programs. But the film and TV worlds are also now staffed and headed, to a greater degree than ever before, by college-trained men and women. Even Hollywood agents these days more often than not have university degrees, although they rarely post their diplomas on their office walls.

There are many ramifications of this evolving relationship between academic and professional worlds. For many years a national collegiate drama festival has been held in Washington, D.C., offering wide recognition to college actors through the Irene Ryan acting award. Many

college-connected professional theatres, some operating in the summertime and some during the school year, now provide "half-way"
employment situations where students can work with professionals.
Apprenticeships and internships now connect several university drama
departments with nearby or on-campus professional companies, and
offer seasonal opportunities for students to act with, study with, and
rub elbows with professional actors on a regular basis. Sometimes even
union membership credits can be obtained in the process. All these
factors favor university training as a base for the emerging actor's
career.

But not all is wonderful in university drama departments, and
there are several things you must watch out for.

Perhaps the most important thing is that the university environment, even under the best circumstances, is an amateur one—and
sometimes it is amateurish as well. Universities have a disproportionate
number of young people, and university directors often cast young
people in older roles. This can create a resigned attitude with regard to
casting standards: The production will aspire only to a minimal level of
competence, a level that is "all that can be achieved under the circumstances." There is no harm in this unless it drags down your *own* standards, which, unfortunately, it is likely to do. Audiences in the
professional theatre are not as indulgent of circumstances, and not as
amused by the often-affected performances of adolescents as aged
kings, queens, and master builders. Performing such roles may not be
all that good for you, either.

In addition, there is a back-patting coziness in many drama departments that can lull student actors into a false sense of security, prevent-
ing them from developing their craft in a disciplined manner, and
encouraging them to rest on yet ill-deserved laurels. Many students
come to New York with their M.F.A.'s in hand and glowing reviews in
their portfolio, but with slender skills, sketchily developed and only
casually tested against a too-easily-won campus popularity.

There are also many campus drama instructors, academically
trained, who (consciously or unconsciously) resent the professional
theatre world; and there are others, professionally experienced, who
have fled the professional world in anger or bitterness. Both can badly
misrepresent the profession.

And finally, there are a few programs that are simply bad, out of
touch with the profession, professing to teach what they know nothing
about.

How should you pick a good college or graduate drama school?
How do you avoid a hopelessly antiquated or inadequate one? Ask

around, of course, and get recommendations from teachers, school counselors, and professional actors and directors. Look at the catalogues of major universities. No one would quarrel with the notion that the Yale Drama School in New Haven and the Juilliard School in New York are the most celebrated academic acting schools in the country, and have produced a great share of our leading actors, but there are many other outstanding institutions. Each January *U.S. News and World Report* publishes an annual survey (*America's Graduate Schools*) that purports to rank the top twenty graduate drama programs in the country. The *ARCO Guide to Performance Arts Programs*, published by Prentice-Hall every two or three years, seeks to rank the top ten or fifteen, focusing on acting programs in particular. Many of the country's leading departments are in the University/Resident Theatre Association (URTA), which holds collective auditions for admission: If you are nominated by your school and successfully pass a local screening audition, you can be seen by all of them at the same time in any of three sites around the United States. And many of these programs, and many others, advertise in journals: *American Theatre* and *Back Stage/Back Stage West* most prominently. The *Back Stage* annual College Guide, published in mid-November as an insert, included eighty-three ads for college drama programs—plus a half dozen dance programs—in 1996.

If you're interested in a drama school, read the ads, read the catalogues in your library, and write to the schools that interest you. *Visit* the three or four departments that seem most suitable to your interest and finances. *Write* to the departments that interest you and let them know you're coming. Ask to *see* both faculty-directed and student-directed productions, if that can be arranged. Ask to visit an acting class. Hang around the bulletin board—there is *always* a bulletin board—and talk to the students you see there. Try to get the inside picture. Wherever you will go, you'll be there for a long while, so get active in your search. Find out as much as you can before committing your time and money.

Some things to look for in choosing a theatre school:

- A faculty with *professional experience*. At least some of the faculty in acting should be professional actors or directors, preferably in a variety of acting media.

- A faculty *presently involved* in professional theatre; or a program with active apprenticeships in professional theatre. You want to be taught up-to-date techniques, and you want to work with people who have professional contacts themselves.

- An *organized plan* for the training of actors. A fine acting program is not merely a collection of fine actors revealing the secrets of

their craft. A good program has a working methodology, or peda-
gogy, with various courses directly feeding into each other so that
you will graduate with integrated and comprehensive training, not
just a mish-mash of information and critiques.

- *Proximity* to ongoing professional theatre activity. This means
  within commuting distance of New York or Los Angeles, or at least
  near a city (or cities) with more than one resident professional
  company. You should have the opportunity to view professional
  work at more than one theatre, and with frequency, and to see it in
  relation to your own work.

- *Facilities, staff, and budgets* sufficient to ensure quality work at all levels. This does not mean that the college or university must boast a
  battery of multimodal theatres with computer lightboards and
  hydraulic stages (although some do). It does mean that works put
  on by the department must be respectable, and not prefaced by
  bundles of apologies or disclaimers. It also means a hardworking
  and energetic staff, willing to put in time with you.

- *Good student morale.* Drama students traditionally gripe to each
  other, yet put on shining faces to outsiders. Both behaviors indicate healthy morale. Watch out for any program where the students are unwarrantedly complacent or openly bitter.

- Opportunities to study *dance* and *voice* (singing) as well as acting.
  Stage actors particularly should seek as much training in music theatre as possible because more and more contemporary stage plays
  demand musical abilities. Since versatility is important for every
  stage actor, you should find and take every opportunity to enlarge
  your performing repertoire. Check also for opportunities to learn
  stage combat, mime, period movement, and audition technique.

- Opportunities to study *classical* acting. You may not think Shakespeare is your metier, but you should study it anyhow. The training
  may come in handy five years down the road, and besides, you
  might discover a talent you never imagined you possessed. Most
  LORT theatres do regular productions of the classics, at least once
  a year. Your ability to perform Shakespeare or Molière will certainly be a strong point in your favor when you compete for an
  apprenticeship or for a paid position with these companies.

- Opportunities to work *on camera.* Some universities have videotape
  facilities or complete TV studios where you can learn to work on
  camera, and study how to hit your marks while playing a scene. You
  *can* learn this later, but a school that provides such opportunities
  gives you a chance to get a jump on the competition.

- *A showcase performance* in either New York or Los Angeles—or both —which presents the graduates' work to professional agents and casting directors. Some forty schools now provide such graduate showcases.

- A strong *alumni placement* record. What are the program's recent graduates actually doing? What percent of the last three classes are actually working actors, or have agents, or have become members of acting unions? You should feel free to ask. Good programs should be able to document the success of a reasonable percentage of their recent grads. You should be able to get real information about this—actual alumni names and their professional credits—not just vague statements. (I was once asked to evaluate a university's "professional actor training" M.F.A. program at which, after saying, "Our graduates work in theatres all over the country," the program head could not actually identify a *single graduate* of the past ten years who had become a union professional actor. I recommended the program be closed, and it was.)

- *Superior work.* Above all, be sure the school productions look good. The level of acting should be at your level or better. Don't ever go to a school because you think you'll have an easy chance to walk off with the starring roles there. You want the *best* possible school, the *best* possible teachers, and the *best* possible fellow students. You might as well start getting used to high-level competition; you'll face it from now on.

A final word about college: While you're there, don't waste your time. Study, of course, all the theatre you can. Learn to sing and dance—learn ballet, tap, and jazz. Learn to fence. Study literature, history, psychology, politics, economics, philosophy. These things will not only feed your art, they will feed you. As actress Suzanne Pleshette says, "Make sure you have a real life, other interests, things that fill you, because if you only live when you're working, you lead a very shallow existence and you have very little to bring back to the work." Actors these days are smart and they are active; they branch into writing and directing, they engage in politics, they teach. As the late Duncan Ross, former artistic director of the Seattle Repertory Theatre, said, "There is no such thing as a good actor who is unintelligent." Train, yes, but also *learn*: Use, explore, and expand your mind.

## Professional Classes

Professional classes refer to a collection of schools and teachers, mainly in New York and Los Angeles, that teach acting (and often related theatre disciplines) for set fees. These institutions and individuals are not affiliated with universities, and do not ordinarily offer subjects unrelated to theatre.

The number of professional acting schools and studios has increased tremendously in the past twenty-five years. *Back Stage West's* annual *Spotlight on Acting Schools and Coaches* listed nearly 300 in Southern California alone in 1996; there are at least as many in New York, and probably another three or four hundred scattered elsewhere around the country. They're easy to find: Many advertise in the weekly trade papers on both coasts, and many more are described and sometimes even rated in various publications available in drama bookstores when you get into town (see the appendix).

Professional schools and teachers vary enormously in the nature of their offerings and in the quality of their instruction. Some are full drama schools, providing comprehensive theatre education. Others are schools devoted to a single teacher's method of self-expression. Others are specialized academies for certain skills: camera acting, TV commercials, improvisation, voiceovers, stage speech, comedy, singing, dance, audition technique, and the like. Many schools and teachers offer a variety of courses and classes; including, usually, a basic acting sequence plus a variety of specialized workshops. Naturally the comprehensive schools are geared to the student without prior dramatic training, while the independent teachers and class offerings are more suitable to the university-trained actor located in New York or Los Angeles. Specialized classes provide a source of continuing education for actors, and are very much part of the actor's life, even after roles start coming in. Internationally known actors frequently show up in acting classes in New York and Hollywood to refresh their skills and learn new ones.

Finding a professional class is tricky because, unlike universities and colleges, there is no system of regular outside accreditation, and professional schools go in and out of business—sometimes as often as the teachers go in and out of acting roles. Look at the ads, get recommendations, interview the directors, and ask to audit a class. Talk to current students. Remember, professional acting classes live through your tuition, and their advertisements and recruitment techniques are designed to make you *think* the classes are indispensable to your future. Beware of *any* acting teachers who imply that studying with them guarantees professional employment; this is actually *illegal* in California, although it hasn't prevented hundreds of innuendos to that effect from being widely circulated by too-hungry instructors. Watch out also for acting classes that require you to pay for several months in advance, or to pay for management services, photographs, or separate showcases to which "important casting directors" will be invited, or that market themselves as "star search" agencies. Virtually all of these are scams. "The Search for New Stars Is Happening Now" trumpeted an ad in *Teen, Seventeen,* and *Cosmopolitan* magazines a few years back. The studio ad promised "you'll be auditioned on camera [and] interviewed by some of the top acting and modeling 'career makers' who will be there to judge you. We're looking for girls who want to be the 'new stars' of the '90's." What the ad was really offering was simply a $2,100 acting course with no guarantee of professional visibility; the studio was sued by the Los Angeles Attorney's Office's Consumer Protection Unit and paid a settlement in 1995 of $50,000; it no longer exists. The best courses and teachers are frank in their advertising, fair in their prices, honest in their evaluation of your potential (and your chances), and aboveboard in their registration and tuition policies. Don't be afraid to ask questions and don't be willing to accept less than complete answers.

Who should study at professional schools? Probably just about everybody. The main advantage of the professional school is that it is right in the midst of professional activity, it is run by professionals with "real world" values dominating every classroom exercise and discussion, and your fellow students will be like-minded professional aspirants. Full training programs, such as the Neighborhood Playhouse School of the Theatre in New York (founded by the late, legendary acting teacher, Sandy Meisner) and the American Academy of Dramatic Arts (the oldest acting school in the English-speaking world, founded in 1884 and operating on both coasts) are well-designed for the high school graduate, offering year-long and multi-year training programs. Intensive month-by-month sessions, as are offered by the HB Studio in New York (founded by the late Herbert Berghof and run by his wife, Uta Hagen) and the Film Actors Workshop in Hollywood (founded by CBS producer Tony Barr and run by Eric Kline) are excellent for professional, practical training beyond the academy and/or the M.F.A. There are also schools and studios run by well-known actors (Nina Foch, Kim Darby), by writers on acting (Ned Manderino, Eric Morris), and by the official disciples of famous (but deceased) gurus (the Stella Adler Academy of Acting, the [Lee] Strasberg Theatre Institute). Many of these schools will begin by "retraining" you—suggesting (sometimes quite fervidly) that you "unlearn" your collegiate technique in favor of the teacher's style. Go along with it. You never really unlearn anything anyway, and it's what you *do* learn that's going to count.

When you get into a professional class, as you should as soon as you hit New York or Los Angeles, get right to work, and work hard. Commercial schools do not have grades or examinations; there is no motivation for study except your own drive to learn. Hard work and energy, not money, is your main investment. You will get out of these classes precisely what you put into them—a cliché perhaps, but one that is never so true as in an acting class. Meet the other people in the class and get to know them; they will be your first contacts in the professional world that you wish to enter.

## Apprenticeships

Apprenticeship programs are a third possible training ground for actors, and the best of these offer excellent opportunities for professional development—when you can get them.

Apprenticeships (or internships, as they are sometimes called) put you in direct daily contact with working professionals, and usually have you working side by side with them. Some offer acting classes in addition, and some even offer credits toward union membership under Equity's Membership Candidate program. You will ordinarily pay for room and board, and you may pay a tuition fee as well, although in some cases these may be negotiated if the company wants you and your skills badly enough.

The best apprenticeships are at those LORT theatres that offer seasonal and year-round programs. Some of these apprenticeships are operated in conjunction with university drama departments, such as the joint programs of the Yale Drama School with the Yale Repertory Theatre, or of Florida State University with the Asolo Theatre. A LORT theatre apprenticeship can provide you with the fifty weeks of work necessary to qualify for an Equity card (see the section on unions in the next chapter), as well as a sound education in professional theatre practice. Summer theatre programs at outstanding resident stock theatres, such as Williamstown and Stockbridge in Massachusetts, are also great training grounds for professional actors, as has been demonstrated over past decades. You can find information about apprenticeships through summer theatre publications (see the appendix), through the University/Resident Theatre Association, and by writing directly to professional theatre companies that you know have such programs, or that you think might be interested in creating one.

## A Word of Caution

One final cautionary word about preprofessional training: It can be overdone. College, acting classes, and the local community theatre can be very comfortable places. A lovely security envelops you: You are known, liked, respected, and well reviewed by the locals and by your teachers. But check your goals. If you want to move on, you had better go when you are ready rather than hang around merely because it is safe. Recognize the point of stagnation when the competition gets soft. There are actors who become so devoted to a favorite drama school or drama teacher that they study for eight or ten years without going to a single audition, on the grounds that they are "not ready." The "professional student" is really psychologically aberrant. Recognize this trait in yourself, if it exists, and fight it. When you are ready to take the plunge, take it. The proper time is something only you can decide upon.

## CONTACTS

Here we are. Contacts are the nemesis of the young unknown actor. You can whine, gripe, yell, and complain about it, but contacts are important—*vital*—in getting jobs in the theatre. But do not just give up on this account: *Think.* What does the term "contacts" actually mean?

Contacts are the people you know and who know you. Switch sides for a moment. If you were casting a play in a hurry and knew that Harry was "just right" for the role, wouldn't you call Harry and ask him to audition? Would you really search through the drama classes at Amalgamated State University to find out if there were somebody else as good? No. You would call Harry and say, "Harry, I've got a part that's just right for you." And Harry would come over and read it, and if you liked his reading you would cast him in the role. It's not that you owe Harry a favor, but you like Harry, you envision Harry doing the part, and you can settle the matter in a quick, friendly way. Well, maybe you are the one in a thousand who wouldn't call Harry, but the other 999 are in New York and Hollywood casting offices right now. You can either moan about it or work to become Harry. The choice is yours.

There is nothing mysterious about "contacts," and it is fruitless to play sour grapes and say "I can't get anywhere because I don't have any pull." Of course you don't, but neither does anybody else just starting out. It is not as though your competition all went to school with Tom

Cruise or swam in Julia Roberts's pool. Everybody, or almost every-body, starts off just as unknown and unwanted as you. If you don't have contacts, you just have to develop some. It is as simple as that.

But wait a minute, you say. You don't *accept* that "it's who you know, not what you know." You want to make it "on your own." Well, what does *that* mean? That you will be discovered? Where? In your acting class? Singing in the shower? The fact is that NOBODY ever makes it on his or her "own." It always takes *somebody else*, and that somebody else is your contact.

This is no time to play around with semantics. Getting jobs in the-atre involves getting people to know you and know your work. These people are your contacts, and if you are good enough, and develop enough of them, one of them will pay off for you. And then it doesn't matter if you got introduced because he was your uncle's cousin or your drama teacher's drama teacher. Someone sees you, likes you, and hires you. How else do you expect it to happen?

Most hirings in the theatre and film world are, in fact, done among a network of acquaintances and friends—not *all* of it, but *most* of it. Why? Because, all else being equal (and most of the time, all else *is* equal), directors and producers prefer to work with actors they have worked with before over those they have never seen. And they would rather see people they know than total strangers. You have to break into the network, and you have to get contacts.

And now, who said you have no contacts? *Everybody you know* is a potential contact. The actor in the community play with you might next year be producing a film; your college drama instructor might be directing a play; your aunt might have a friend who has just written a TV show. It is to your advantage to get to know people in the business. Who knows what they might be doing in a month or so? Many actors mail postcards to everyone they know every four to six months, just to stay in the network. Such networking is not presumptuous: It is appre-ciated, and it works.

The important contacts you presumably do not know yet, but you will. Every time you audition you meet at least one. At every interview you meet secretaries, directors, and other actors. These meetings can be forgotten in an instant, but if you are personable and they are intrigued by you, a contact is made. You don't have to be pushy. Phony friendliness and phony friends are the most loathsome aspect of show business, and it is easy to completely misplay your hand in this way. Theatre people are the worst name-droppers in the world and "Oh, he's a good friend of mine," becomes a line that is too frequently applied to a person met once five years ago. But you can build your real network of contacts—the people who know you and know your work—by simply and modestly finding ways to keep your friends aware of you. And you can keep aware of *them*, by writing down in a little black book the names of everyone you meet, so that the next time you see them you can remember their names and what they do.

Remember these fundamental principles about contacts:

- No *one* contact is going to make it for you, and the fact that somebody else knows somebody important is not going to make it for him or her, either. Everyone you know can help you by trading information, tips, advice, and, ultimately, offers of employment.

- People you have known for years and who have subsequently "made it" may not help you out at all. That is not just because success has made them indifferent to their old pals. Many genuinely try to follow the suggestion of Edith Piaf, who said that when you reach the top you should throw the ladder back down for everybody else. But your newly arrived friends are not as secure as they seem. In fact, they are in a particularly vulnerable position. Even if they can help you, they may not want to risk suggesting you to *their* higher-ups, fearing that if you fail, they'll fall. Beyond this, they may question their earlier evaluation of you now that they have new surroundings and a new perspective. They would rather you made it on your own—then they could be *sure*. This is small comfort, of course, but you will probably have to live with it.

- Contacts may not look like contacts. The mousy-looking man hanging around backstage might just be getting ready to film *Grandson of Batman*, and is looking you over for a part. Be yourself and make friends; it can't hurt you.

- Contacts may not *act* like contacts. People who give out jobs in show business are so besieged they frequently hide the fact behind a veil of feigned clumsiness and innocence. Play along.

- All kinds of people will *tell* you that they are contacts. They're probably not. Maybe they are just nice and want to help, and maybe they are after you for other reasons. Some just like to sound important. Treat everybody the same, and stay a bit skeptical.

A word about sleeping with the producer. If you are a talented, personable, charming, and sexy person, there will be all sorts of people interested in casting you. And there will also be all sorts of people interested in going to bed with you. But these will quite possibly not be the same people.

A cartoon that used to hang outside the Screen Gems casting office window shows a young girl dressing in a bedroom and calling to an older man, "Now, when are you going to make me a star?" The older man is in the next room, smiling and cutting her a paper star.

Let's not be prudish, though. It is illogical to assume that if the casting director is your intimate he or she won't be working a little harder for you than for others who come in for interviews. It is equally obvious that if your bed partner is a studio executive, all things are not going to be equal when it comes to casting the next show. Writer/director Paul Sylbert does admit in his biting Hollywood exposé *Final Cut* that he was pressured to cast the mistress of an AVCO/Embassy executive in his film, *The Steagle*. But the larger point is that when the poor lady proved unequal to the (acting) challenge, she was fired, to everybody's chagrin and the actress's mortification. Nobody gets a real job or builds a career *simply* by going from one studio bed or casting couch to another; not anymore at least. And why not? New awareness —and legal implications—of sexual harassment have put a damper on sexual tradeoffs. "You never, *never* interview a woman in anything other than a very open situation," says Mike Fenton, one of Hollywood's best —and best-known—casting directors, who keeps a woman assistant at his side whenever he interviews a female client. Potential sexually transmitted diseases, scandal in the tabloids, and the inevitable loss of self-esteem are probably also inhibiting factors. Most important, however, the great passion of the entertainment industry is for success, not sex, which is readily available in any case. And the great fear is failure. No producer, director, or casting director would casually put his or her show, or career, at risk just for a little playtime. Everyone in the business is working too hard and has too much at stake for that. "These days, sleeping one's way to oblivion is more likely than sleeping one's way upward. Marry them—or date out of town," says celebrated producer Lynda Obst (*The Fisher King, Sleepless in Seattle*) in her apt and penetrating *Hello, He Lied*. Everybody's working too hard, anyway, Obst explains. "Men are exhausted and enervated, while women are doing hundreds of military push-ups in aerobics classes." So: Forget it.

## COMMITMENT AND WILL TO SUCCEED

Your power supply is your sense of commitment and your will to succeed. They will keep you going despite the thousand and one ego reversals you are bound to encounter. As a young, professional actor explains, the greatest danger you face is going "DEAF—depressed, envious, aching, and frustrated." It is your commitment and sheer persistence that will vanquish DEAFness if anything can, that will keep you going through poverty and loneliness, when your friends are marrying and having kids and making money and you are eating out of cans on the Lower East Side waiting for your ship to come in. You must continue to hang in there, to train yourself, to get information, to develop contacts. To do all these things, you must have an overwhelming desire for success. It is often said that the people who make it in the theatre are simply those who want it badly enough.

It is not necessary to step on other people's toes, to do zany things that draw attention to yourself, or to alienate friends, relatives, and competitors in your quest for success. But quest for it you must. Getting started in theatre means *initiating* actions: getting on the telephone and on the pavement, looking up people, calling on strangers, getting to places at 6 A.M. and waiting around for three hours—all sorts of indelicate and unappetizing tasks. It also means weeks, months, even years of frustration, failure, defeat, and simple boredom. It means sitting around waiting for the telephone to ring when it has not rung in months. These things are at best unpleasant and at worst may lead you to the brink of suicidal depression. Only a massive will to succeed will overcome them. The commitment must be strong, persistent, and all-encompassing. All sorts of personal sacrifices must be assumed. "The only secret," says Jon Lovitz, "is to keep getting better and persisting." Lovitz spent seven years after college trying to get a "first break," working as a messenger while his friends were becoming doctors and lawyers. "I was getting shit from my father and wondering if I hadn't made a giant mistake," he remembers. But the persistence, and his relentless self-improvement, has paid off handsomely.

Nobody knows how long it will take to "make" you an actor. It is best to set yourself some sort of time schedule—most actors do. Five years is an average allotment, five years after the first day that you say to yourself, "I am now an actor, and I'm available for work." Five years from the day you hit the pavements, the studios, the agencies—from the day you decide that whatever you are doing, you will drop it to get the first job.

From that day on, you scrimp on money for gifts, for food, for furniture, for an apartment. You spend money on pictures, a telephone service, resumes, acting classes, membership in a health club, and some good clothes for auditions. You get the sleep you need and the medication and exercise you need; you're going to have to be ready to look terrific on an hour's notice any day of the week. You direct your time, your money, and your energy to two things: learning acting and getting work. Whatever is left over goes to less important things like your social life or your marriage. Yes, less important. If you aren't 100% committed to your career, you will be passed over by someone who is.

And if you succeed, you still haven't "made it." "Listen, my dear," the late actress Ruth Gordon said to her *Harold and Maude* co-star Bud Cort, "you *never* make it. I'm on that phone twelve hours a day. I make it happen for myself, you're gonna make it happen for yourself. No one makes it." An actor never relaxes, because an actor—even a star— is always out of work, always looking for the next job. "You can't hang onto your laurels," said veteran James Earl Jones, discussing his profession. "Actors do not have choices, do not have claims, just because they are considered stars. I'm a troubadour, going from castle to castle looking for an open door through which to walk and sing for my supper. That's the way it is; it never changes."

But there's nothing grim about this. A committed attitude, such as that personified by Ruth Gordon and James Earl Jones, carries with it something more than just a pragmatic advantage in selling yourself on the job market. Exciting people are committed people—in art, in politics, or in life. And it is to your advantage to be exciting.

So be dedicated. It will offend the weak, but it will inspire others. A life of dedication (to your art, hopefully, but even to yourself) is fulfilling; it galvanizes your talents and directs your energies. It characterizes all great artists of all times. As Bernard Shaw wrote:

> This is the true joy in life, the being used for a purpose recognized by yourself as a mighty one: the being thoroughly worn out before you are thrown on the scrap heap, the being a force of Nature instead of a feverish selfish little clod of ailments and grievances, complaining that the world will not devote itself to making you happy.

So live as if you meant it, and become an artist in the same way. This involves a little presumptuous egotism; flow with it. Michelangelo, Beethoven, Bernhardt, Heifetz, Toscanini, Callas, Aeschylus: All great artists have been persons of great dedication and temperament, persons who have sacrificed easy-going pleasantness to the drive for perfection that has welled up inside them. If you are determined to make it as an actor, you are living life at high stakes anyway. You might as well go all the way with it.

## ATTITUDE, DISCIPLINE, AND CAPACITY FOR PSYCHOLOGICAL ADJUSTMENT

How crippling are the comments, "He has a bad attitude!" or "She's undisciplined." They keep talented performers out of work and get them places on informal, rumor-fed blacklists that they may not truly deserve. The slightest whisper, from one associate producer to another, that "we've got enough problems in this show without dealing with *hers!*" is frequently the last exchange before "Thanks very much, dear. We'll be in touch with you if anything comes up."

It may be desirable to be daffy, but it is death to be genuinely crazy, or have casting people think you are. Crazy people are hard to contact, don't show up on time, forget their lines and their blocking, annoy other actors, antagonize directors, defy wardrobers, and in general are far more trouble than they are worth. If you are crazy, hide it. If you aren't, please don't pretend to be.

But mental health means more than merely being on the near side of psychosis. To be relatively stable, well-balanced, gregarious, and sensitive to the plights of others is a valuable asset. But there are more specific ways in which your attitude can work for you or against you.

Perhaps the worst attitude—the most destructive one—that appears commonly in young actors is the one that says, "I'm waiting to be discovered." This is a complex neurosis, and its effects are virtually fatal. Actors with this attitude are afraid of trying, afraid of looking foolish, afraid of failing. They never contact agents, never set up interviews, and never discuss career plans or goals with anyone but close friends. Considering self-promotion callous, these actors dedicate their time to perfecting some small aspect of their craft. Secretly, such actors hope that some unknown benefactor will find them in their hidden places of work and sign them to giant film contracts. But they will never take the initiative because that would soil their "purity."

One must beware of this attitude because it masks itself under seemingly noble forms. Basically it is simple fear. It is also egotism: the belief that one's own talent is so obvious that it need only be seen once to be instantly appreciated and called into demand. It is also romanticism: No Hollywood movie about the birth of a star has ever shown the aspirant plowing through the yellow pages or passing hours in the waiting rooms of an agent's office. The heroine has been discovered by the producer who visits the little summer stock theatre, or has been an understudy who is called on at the last moment to replace the aging star. The fact is that it takes plain work to get work in return, and *you* must go out and do the work because nobody is going to do it for you.

Another attitude that will hurt you if you overplay it is obvious disdain for the role, play, or medium for which you are auditioning. For example, it is not hard to find dozens of people working on a television show that will grumble about its lack of artistic integrity. Be careful about jumping on this particular bandwagon. Most people working in the theatre, films, or television *like* what they are doing, at least while they're doing it. At the very least they persuade themselves they like doing it. You may never watch a TV show yourself, but if you are reading for *Melrose Place,* it won't help you to take a superior attitude to the art of television or to the premises of the program. The producers, directors, and actors are all intelligent, sensitive people. They probably have pride in what they are doing, even if they don't always act like it. To mock the show mocks them, so don't be led into following their self-deprecating remarks. Every director would prefer to cast an actor who will appreciate the role, the play, and the medium.

Discipline is a primary ingredient in the professional actor's attitude. In fact, discipline is usually considered the chief distinction between the amateur and the professional. Good colleges, commercial schools, and community theatres insist on it, but these are in a minority. Discipline means that for the entire period between your first call and your dismissal you are concentrating on your tasks as an actor to the exclusion of everything else. It means you are always on time or early for every call: *not just usually, but always.* There is absolutely no reason for an actor to be even one minute late to a single audition, rehearsal, or makeup call—whether you're a star or an extra. As Maureen Stapleton puts it, "Actors are the only people, good or bad, hot or cold, who show up on time."

Promptness means you are always there and ready to do what you are asked, and that all your acting instruments—voice, body, imagination, and intelligence—are at the disposal of the director every moment you are on call.

Not that it is always easy to see this in a professional situation. If you have the chance to watch the taping of a television show, you will see actors lounging around, talking to each other, joking on the set, drinking coffee, dropping lines during takes, and generally exhibiting an air of nonchalance. What you will also observe, however, is the immediate attention that the director can command, and how within a matter of five seconds twenty-five people will snap into total concentration and readiness. The nonchalance is necessary relaxation, but it is superficial. These are professionals, conditioned like flight crews to an ever-ready professional alertness. Until you are experienced enough to have one eye always open to the job at hand, concentrate fully on what you are doing. If you don't, you might find yourself still laughing at some joke by the coffeepot while everybody else has suddenly reappeared on the set and the director is calling your name. In a rage. Artistic temperament can be a drive for perfection and impatience with inefficiency, or it can mask your inexperience and demonstrate your lack of discipline. It's obviously to your advantage to be easy to work with. "The reason I will use actors from last year's festival is that I know I can work with them," said former California Shakespeare Festival artistic director Mark Lamos (now artistic director at the Hartford Stage Company). "I don't care for temperament at all. I don't need egos. I want real pros."

Discipline includes a willingness to take direction. No good director will become offended or irritated by genuine questions or discussion about blocking, emphasis, or motivation, but continual complaints such as "It doesn't feel right," particularly when they are obviously meant to cover insecurity, drive directors up the wall and may land you out of a job—sometimes right then and there. Among professionals, an inability to take direction may become your most talked-about liability, and unless you are sure that your presence in the play or film will draw thousands of paying spectators, you cannot afford that reputation.

The major cliché in director-actor hassles may be mentioned here, although if you have been in any theatre in America you have already heard it. That is when the "old school" director (say, the late George Abbot) tells the "method" actor (say, Marlon Brando) to cross left, and the actor mulls it over and asks, "What's my motivation?" "Your paycheck!" retorts the director. Nothing in today's theatre is that cut and dried, however. The director-actor relationship must be a balanced one, and both artists must genuinely desire to work well together for it to succeed. Obviously, since you are the one who is starting out, you have to do your part *plus*, despite possible disagreements.

In short, your attitude should be positive and infectious. You like the part, you like the play, you like the medium, you like the director and the direction, and you want like hell to do it and do it well. Nobody ever really gets offended at an actor who is genuinely eager, unless that eagerness pushes everybody else off the set. No director is offended by an actor, for example, who reads the play before auditions and memorizes half-a-dozen roles, and who communicates the genuine feeling that he will work like crazy if he gets the part; professional theatre art, behind the scenes, isn't at all casual. While you must never cross over the line by noisily and obsequiously flattering the producers, a clear tone of enthusiasm for the project is bound to be in your favor, and notes of ironic weariness or indifference to it will work powerfully (albeit silently) against you.

## FREEDOM FROM ENTANGLEMENTS AND INHIBITIONS

Freedom is complex and it does not exist in the absolute. Everyone is bound by restraints: practical, financial, social, and mental. Success in the pursuit of an acting career requires minimizing, not utterly eliminating, these restraints.

An actor must be free to audition for roles and to accept employment when and where it is offered. The important job offer can come at an awkward time (in the archetypal Hollywood story it always comes as the actor is about to leave on a honeymoon) and can send you to an inconvenient location. You must be free to accept it, however.

Commitment to an acting career means frequent (or at least occasional) slacking-off on other commitments, particularly those to husbands and wives, babies, friends, parents, outside employers, and teachers. Obviously it is better if you can arrange your priority of commitments in such a way that your career plans may proceed unhindered.

Naturally there will be some conflicts of interest here. You are an actor, but you are also a human being in a society, and you have friends, family, and all sorts of people whose plans and whose feelings will affect yours. After all, there are 8,760 hours in a year, and even a fully employed actor will spend 7,000 of them away from the set; if you have alienated all your friends just to be at the beck and call of every agent and producer in the business, you are apt to spend a lot of lonely hours by the TV set.

The only thing you can do is to come completely to grips with the nature of the business you are trying to enter and make certain that people who may depend on you are aware of it, too—and are also sympathetic to your ambitions. They may not be. Many actors who know the score vow never to marry another actor. An actor is rarely the model wife or husband of whom Dear Abby would be proud. As an actor, you will be subject to an ever-changing, unpredictable schedule;

you will be on call for location work in New Dehli or New Haven while
your spouse is taking care of the house and babies; you will be facing
the terrific frustration of looking for parts and breaks in an industry
where unemployment is routine; you will be sacrificing much of your
income for classes and workshops and hundreds of photos and postcards of your lovely self; and finally, when you do start to get work, you
will be deeply involved in the emotional crises, love affairs, and strange
psychologies of the characters you are given to play. Face it: You're no
prize. And face realistically the trials your relationship will inevitably
endure.

Should an actor get married at all? Well, it is far beyond the scope
of this little book to recommend one way or the other, and it is also
doubtful that any recommendation here would be very seriously considered anyway. However, it is obvious that marriage *can* become a serious entanglement to a stage or film career if both of you fail to
understand what you are getting into. If you marry without such an
understanding, either you will completely frustrate your spouse and
your marriage will end up in ruins, or you will frustrate yourself and
your career will end up in ruins. You are no doubt already aware that
the acting profession has a ridiculously high divorce rate. For some
people it is an either/or situation. In a candid interview, Shelley Winters explained, "You see, honey, you've got to really make a choice in
life. It's either a good role or a good marriage. . . . I guess I love working more than being married . . . so I gave up this great guy for this
great role." And so it goes: You probably *can't* have everything.

And there's the financial matter. You can't be sure of supporting
anyone, including yourself. Ideally, a young actor should marry only if
he or she is rich or working—or marrying someone else who is. And an
actor should marry only someone who understands the rigors of the
career. Having said this, we rest our case. There are, after all, more
than pragmatic considerations in this matter.

There are other entanglements besides marriage, of course. Some
are financial, some emotional. You may be unwilling or unable to move
around, to work with certain kinds of people, or to play certain kinds
of parts. You may object to undressing in front of the camera (or an
audience), or performing in a way you find undignified. There is a line
you must draw for yourself here, but naturally the lower that line (that
is, the fewer your inhibitions) the more "available" you are. Insofar as
that line now must be drawn to include or exclude doing nude scenes
(which occur in numerous movies), you will have to be prepared to
define your views on this issue if you plan to work in films. There is,
however, one "inhibition" that is known as "taste." An actor *must* be

inhibited from doing things that are tasteless and unrewarding. Performing in the nude for a major art film and for a one-day stag movie obviously have different values, both as a creative act and as a step in your professional career. A young actor who is 100% available to do a blue film for a $100 fee may find himself or herself unusable for anything *but* that in the future. As Georgina Spelvin, the undraped star of *The Devil in Miss Jones,* has made clear, "Be aware, girls, if you make the choice to go into explicit pictures, it's for life."

## GOOD INFORMATION AND ADVICE

You will need the most current information and the most up-to-date advice if you are to pursue a career successfully. This book may be filled with information and advice, but, like any book, it was written at least a year before you're reading it. You need to know the day-by-day, and sometimes hour-by-hour, developments in your prospective field.

### The Trade Journals

Both the theatre and film worlds have trade journals—universally known as "the trades"—that report on what's happening. In New York the venerable *Variety* and *Back Stage,* both weeklies, report on all acting media: stage, screen, TV, and high-tech interactives. In Hollywood you can count on the New York spin-offs of *Daily Variety* (a slick daily, mainly about film and TV) and *Back Stage West* (about all media), plus the independent trades *Hollywood Reporter* (another slick daily, also film/TV oriented) and *Drama-Logue* (a slick weekly, covering all media).

Not all of these trades are equally helpful to the actor, however. Both the *Hollywood Reporter* and the two *Varieties* are addressed primarily to producers and theatre owners; if you subscribe to any of them you will mainly be reading about corporate mergers, executive comings and goings, and who's selling their Maine or Malibu mansions for four million six.

*Drama-Logue* and the two *Back Stages,* however, are addressed directly to the actor and are filled with casting calls, advice columns, interviews with agents and casting directors, and even advertisements that might come close to fitting your particular needs. Naturally the casting calls are mainly for work that you can't get (auditions for which you must be submitted by an agent) or don't want ("erotic telegram services," nonpaying student films in New Jersey, cattle calls for shows already known to be cast, and so on), but there are always some legitimate opportunities, and even some illegitimate ones you're going to want to know about and investigate further.

Even beyond the casting calls, reading the trades gives you the feeling that you're part of the general goings-on. As such, they help you surmount the natural feeling of alienation and aloneness every newcomer feels when hitting New York or Hollywood for the first time. They *are* the news of show business, and a half hour with any one of them will give you a good vocabulary of names, places, and shows and an idea of what's in the heads of the agents, producers, and casting directors who are active at the moment. The trades give you, at the very least, a vicarious sense of participation, and even a vicarious participation is a good start in a business that considers itself a club. Indeed, reading the trades is part of your dues, whether you do it in a library, over someone's shoulder in the subway, or by sneaking into the members' lobby at Equity headquarters in New York.

## Information on the Internet

You can also find information—including some casting news—on the Internet these days. Websites covering (or claiming to cover) the entertainment industry abound; new ones are created every few weeks. There are also Websites and listserves devoted to theatre scholarship, theatre chats, actor self-marketing, and the like. It is not yet clear, however, how this field is going to develop. Certainly nothing on the Web, at the time this book went to press (early 1997), could be considered comprehensive or authoritative, particularly with regard to casting information. Many sites, created with obvious enthusiasm, have already been abandoned; apparently, though no one has bothered to remove them from the net. Many that remain perpetuate blatantly incorrect information, and few make an effort to prioritize between the important, the trivial, and the downright false. Still, the potential for a major Internet role in the actor-hiring process is gigantic. It seems only a matter of time until both character breakdowns and actor photo-resumes will be routinely shuffling by the millions between agents' and casting offices' computers around the world.

Right now, you can place your toe (if not your photo-resume) in a few very promising waters:

- Playbill On-Line, which may currently be found at http://piano.symgrp.com/playbill/, with its comprehensive daily update on theatre news and reviews from Broadway and the New York theatre, is the nation's premiere theatre site. Playbill also offers, though to a lesser extent, coverage of theatre in the regions and abroad. It lists shows currently playing in New York and elsewhere, offers spotty news on casting opportunities around the country, features an over-the-net ticket-purchase service, and offers several interesting columns—including the excellent "Ask Blair," which is sort of a "Dear Abby" for actors, written by Blair Glaser, a New York actress. Playbill On-Line is a commercial service (it sells ads and takes a commission on ticket sales), but for the time being it is free to all webbers.

- Theatre Central, "The Hub of Theatre on the Internet" as they call themselves, may be found at http://www.theatre-central.com/, or via Playbill On-Line. Theatre Central is also a linking service that connects you to theatre listings and casting news—again on a spotty basis. But Theatre Central also offers links to other theatre sites, particularly regional theatres, Shakespeare festivals, and off-Broadway companies, that might themselves prove very useful for hunting down audition possibilities on a one-to-one basis. It can also connect you to acting union Websites for up-to-the-minute contract information.

Will the Internet take over in the theatre news and casting field? No one knows for sure. Its potential is terrific: It's instant, international, and free (once you have access to a computer and a net connection). But actors tend to be a transient crowd, and not many lug a PC with them on the subway or on road trips. And services that don't bring in any revenue for their creators (as is true for most Websites) often find the steam going clean out of them around holiday seasons; that's why there are so many dead sites on the Web. (Nothing is more dispiriting than seeing a live casting announcement for a show that you know has already opened and closed.) Look for the traditional trade papers to continue to provide the most comprehensive and reliable data in this field for the next decade at least.

## Other Sources of Information

Where *else* do you get information? Talk to people. Actors love to talk about their business—some of them talk about almost nothing else. Acting schools are good places to begin, and theatre bars, particularly in New York (check out Joe Allen's, JR's, and the West Bank Café in the Broadway theatre district) are another. Or simply go to a lot of shows, such as the off-off Broadway workshops in New York or the equity-waiver shows in Los Angeles. Even if you don't know a soul in the production, hang around after the curtain call and wander backstage. If there were actors whose performances you liked, congratulate them (an always-effective calling card) and introduce yourself.

At worst, you will engage in an agreeable little conversation. At best, you will strike up a true and valuable friendship (some of the very best have begun in precisely this manner). And friends, of course, are a very fine source of information, perhaps the best there is. With friends in the trade you can get a feeling for the intangibles that control this emotional and frequently mystical business. You can sense out the tips, the hunches, the possibilities, and the probabilities that determine so much of the day-to-day course of the trade's events. You can get a sense of the feelings of the people in charge, and the people under them. Beware, naturally, of being overly influenced by any single person's likes, dislikes, neuroses, or phobias; be prepared to take comments with several grains of salt. Gradually you will gain a working knowledge of what casting possibilities are hot, which agents are really working for which actors, which producers are open to what kinds of suggestions, and in general what your competition is likely to be.

There are theatre schools that specialize in teaching you "how to audition" and "how to get a job," as well as "how to act." They may be useful. There are also actors' information services, actors' "rap groups," and actors' counseling services that are well-intentioned and often useful. You can find them, as well as public lectures on the actor's life, listed in the advertising sections of the trade papers. Of course, there are always a lot of people willing to take your money in return for "inside" tips and suggestions. With these people, you begin to reach the point of diminishing returns, however. No matter how much you may read or hear about the subject of "making it" in acting, nothing begins to approach the knowledge you get by working toward success yourself. The best way to learn the business is to get started, to participate. The suggestions in this book are designed to help you do that. Once you get your start, you can leave this book behind. You will find that you have access to information much more specifically applicable to your needs.

## LUCK

Luck is placed last on this list simply because there is nothing you can do to get it. Luck is a factor that can outweigh most of the others, and there is nothing to do about it but groan. Shelly Duvall is a perfect example. At the time she was cast in the 1970 film *Brewster McCloud,*

Duvall had never studied acting, had never seen a play, and generally disdained theatre people as "weird." She was a suburban housewife living in Houston, Texas, and she was "discovered" while selling her husband's paintings to people who turned out to be MGM producers. In 1997 she performed in her 22nd film, *Home Fires*. The dream of "discovery" lies deep in the heart of every aspiring performer, but it comes almost as often to those who don't work for it as to those who do. Shirley MacLaine was "discovered" when she was called upon to substitute for Carol Haney in the Broadway musical, *Pajama Game*. Hal Wallis was in the audience, and but for this occurrence, Miss MacLaine might still be hoofing on 45th Street. It also turned out that MacLaine was planning to resign from the show the very night that Haney turned her ankle. But what do *you* do about luck? You don't go to Houston to sell oil paintings; that's for sure. You will have to find your own.

# Chapter 3

# The First Decisions

So, let's assume you have all these qualifications for an acting career that we've mentioned so far. Or you think you have them. You are going to look for work. What do you do now? First, you have to make some very important decisions.

## YOUR GOAL

As with every course of action, you have to begin with a goal. That means two things: choosing a goal (that's the easy part) and *committing yourself* to achieving your goal.

In acting, your long-range career goal is simply to get cast. And cast *professionally*. In a play, a film, a television show, a repertory company, an industrial production, a TV commercial—something that will start off your career, get you into an acting union, and begin what you hope will be a long list of professional acting credits.

Who casts? In your high school, college, or community theatre, the director probably posted try-out notices on a bulletin board or announced them in the local paper. You went to the appointed place, read from the script, and made it into the production. In the professional world, things are quite different.

Professional casting is done by many different people, existing at different levels. Basically, there's you the actor and all the other actors looking for the same job (you're all at level 1), your agent (he or she's at level 2), a casting director (level 3), a director (level 4), and a producer (level 5)—and sometimes there are going to be levels 6, 7, and 8 or more as well. *All* of them have to be on your side—or at least not on somebody else's. There's not always this extensive a hierarchy, of course. You don't always need an agent—certainly not if you can get to see the casting director yourself. And sometimes there's no casting director, and/or the director is also the producer. That's how it usually works in college, and it works sometimes in the big leagues that way too. But not too often.

Here's what usually happens. You get an agent who agrees to "represent" you, often under contract. The agent then submits your name to one or more casting directors for a show or a theatre company. The casting director interviews and/or auditions you, together with a bunch of other actors also submitted by *their* agents, and recommends just a few of you to be seen by the show's or the theatre company's directors and other artistic staff. These directors—who may call you in for further interviews and auditions—select whom they would like for the role or roles available. The producers and their staffs then give their approval to the selection and negotiate—normally with your agent—the terms of a contract. As I say, producers may be at various levels. In a theatre company, the producer is generally the artistic director, who may be concerned with your compatibility (artistic, known work habits) and balance (ethnic, professional level) with other company members making up the season. In TV, you might make it up through the show producer and get axed by the executive producer, or through the EP and get turned down by the network based on a variety of factors from your salary demands to your hair color and the brightness of your teeth. In any event, there's a whole lot of people in the casting business (we call them, simply, "casting people" herein) and a whole lot of casting criteria, and you've got your work cut out for you to impress all of the people with all of their individual interests.

Casting people, professionally, do not post try-out notices on a bulletin board, and they do not normally send out press releases on their auditions. Casting people are not easy to see; often they're not easy even to find. They do not keep open office hours, they do not usually answer their mail (not your mail, anyway), and they most certainly do not pick up their own telephones—at least not the telephones whose numbers you can obtain. They do not return your calls, and, indeed, when they do solicit overtures by mail, they specify, in capital letters and with exclamation points, ABSOLUTELY NO PHONE CALLS!!! How do you see such reclusive folks?

More important, how do you get them to see you? This is your basic problem. Creating the access between you, wanting to get cast, and the casting person who can make that happen is the soul of acting professionally. Getting known, getting seen, getting accepted, getting cast, and getting work: This is the process you must negotiate.

First you must decide where to start. In which *medium.*


## YOUR STARTING MEDIUM

The three main theatrical media are, of course, stage, film, and television. (There is also the possibility of starting out in comedy, nightclub work, or modeling, but you'll have to look elsewhere for guidance on these.)

These main media are divided into subgroups. Stage work can include Broadway and off-Broadway shows, stock and regional repertory companies, outdoor theatres, dinner theatres, industrial productions, cruise ship shows, and guest-artist stints at drama schools and universities. Film acting work largely consists of feature films, plus occasional short features and documentaries. Television can include filmed and taped TV specials, series episodes ("episodic TV" in the trade), movies of the week, series pilots, filmed or taped TV commercials, voiceovers, and live announcing positions. In which medium do you want to start your career? In which medium should you *try* to start your career? Where you will live and what you will do will be defined, in part at least, by your answer to that question.

You can simplify the question somewhat. From the acting point of view, film and TV are pretty much the same, since both involve acting for a camera (and usually a film camera, at that), and both are largely headquartered in Los Angeles. There is a status distinction and some long-term career considerations between the two, of course ("I want to be a performer when I'm 80 years old, and I think television can shorten your acting life very quickly," says Christopher Walken), but from a beginner's point of view you can explore both of them at the same time, and in the same town. The real question is: Stage work or camera work? Which one should you begin with?

You should first seek advice from your teachers and valued critic/friends about the medium that best suits you. In weighing the alternatives open to you, you should take the following points into consideration.

Stage work demands great versatility and projection. Stage actors are called upon to do a wide variety of roles, frequently before a thousand or more people at one sitting. A strong, penetrating voice capable of great subtlety is an *absolute necessity*.

You should have a face that projects emotion without mugging, a body that moves well, and a personality that, without pushing, carries well beyond the footlights. Similarly, you should have a command of verse-speaking and classical acting styles, because most stage careers begin in theatres that produce classical plays. Strong talents in the areas of music and dance are increasingly valuable to the stage actor, though not absolutely necessary.

Above all, the stage actor needs the great intangibles: talent, presence, and timing. You must be able to enunciate the subtlest nuances clearly to huge audiences without looking as if you are reading from a speech textbook, and you must convey the sense of a vibrant personality whether you are playing romantic lead, villain, or village idiot.

If your talents lie, on the other hand, in the area of extremely naturalistic performing, a film or television job will probably be more suitable for a start. Acting before a camera ruthlessly shows up all but the most honest of performers. It virtually eliminates the need for projection, since the microphone can be placed just inches away. It has been said that the film actor is the pawn of the film's technicians: "The cameraman usurps the actor's physical composition, the sound mixer his intonation, and the editor his timing." Thus, for the camera actor it is personality, looks, honesty, and the ineffable "quality" that become premium ingredients.

In general, a person's looks count less in live theatre than in film or TV, mainly because makeup can do much more at fifty feet than in a larger-than-life close-up. Many people who are genuinely plain have had brilliant stage careers but have found it impossible to get work in Hollywood. By contrast, a person who is astonishingly beautiful, or interesting in a unique way, can get film or TV work almost on that basis alone. In Hollywood, you can get cast for your teeth.

Can you choose *both* media? Of course you can, eventually. Actors jump media with great frequency these days, and television performers are now almost as common on Broadway as stage actors are on the big and small screens. But you're not going to start in two media simultaneously, even if you plan to be eventually active in all of them. A journey of a thousand miles begins with a single step, Confucius said. You're going to begin with *one* part in *one* medium, and you should put all your focus into that one—for a start.

## CHOOSING A HOME BASE

Where will you live? As an actor you really have only three choices: New York, Los Angeles-Hollywood, or the spiderweb of regional circuits. These choices involve different kinds of theatrical activity and different lifestyles and business procedures for you.

The big cities are, of course, New York and L.A., and "bi-coastal" actors now share their time between the Big Apple, home of Broadway, off-Broadway, and half of TV's soap operas and commercials; and the Big Orange, production home of the major film studios, most TV producers, and hundreds of professional and quasi-professional stage showcases each year. But before turning to the "big bigs," let's look around the rest of the country first.

## REGIONAL THEATRE: THE LORT CIRCUIT

Regional theatre is very likely where you will start out, and perhaps should start out. First, it probably exists close to home, and/or close to your college or university; you may already attend a few on a regular basis. Second, it's a far more *accessible* professional environment than New York or Los Angeles, and you can contact the artistic staff fairly directly. Regional theatre, unlike the "big bigs," is relatively free from the machinations of agents, managers, associate producers, or other middlemen. Not only is it a good place to start out—many actors find it an equally good place to "end up."

Regional theatre is a general term, and not entirely specific. Generally, one uses it to include the spectrum of nonprofit theatre companies, sometimes called "resident companies," throughout the country (including the nonprofit theatre companies in New York City) plus commercial dinner theatres and stock companies out of New York.

The nonprofit (or "not-for-profit") sector is of the greatest current importance, and has experienced a meteoric growth in the past generation. It now (1997) includes more than 300 theatres—254 constituent and 63 associate—all of professional or semi-professional status, the vast majority operating under union contracts loosely linked under the umbrella organization Theatre Communications Group (TCG). Founded in 1961, when there were only sixteen professional theatre companies existing outside of New York (or even including New York, for that matter), TCG has doubled and redoubled many times since, until virtually every city of importance in the United States has at least one nonprofit theatre presenting productions and hiring actors. Regional theatre is no longer a "movement," as it was when TCG was founded; it is, quite simply, America's national theatre, and the major employer of stage actors in the country. In 1995–96, for example, New York theatre (Broadway, off-Broadway, and their touring productions combined) provided only about 31% of the actor work weeks for the American professional stage. The nonprofit regional sector provided 39%—more than a quarter more. TCG offices are (where else?) in New York City, at 355 Lexington Avenue (New York, NY 10017); the office provides, for a small charge, an annual *Theatre Directory* listing all of TCG's 300-plus members and affiliates.

All nonprofit professional theatres are categorized by the Equity contracts under which they operate. Those theatres linked into the League of Resident Theatres (LORT), and operating under the LORT contracts (there are five categories of contract—A, B+, B, C, and D—depending on the theatre's size), are the cream of the nonprofit crop.

LORT is an association of roughly seventy-five first-class nonprofit professional theatres in the major American cities. You've heard of many of them: the Arena Stage in Washington, D.C., the Guthrie Theatre in Minneapolis, the American Conservatory Theatre in San Francisco, the Long Wharf Theatre in New Haven, the South Coast Repertory Theatre in Costa Mesa, the Seattle Repertory Theatre. LORT theatres ordinarily produce independent work of exceptionally high quality; virtually all the Tony and Pulitzer Prize–winning American plays of the 1980s and 1990s were first mounted by LORT companies.

LORT's association with TCG has given the theatres a national "network" and an international identity, much of which is promoted by their monthly magazine, *American Theater*, which lists current schedules around the country. Many of the LORT theatres have federal grants to pursue experimental work and talent development; some have affiliations with universities, and others have conservatories of their own. In addition to their stage work, many LORT theatres have been invited to have their productions taped for national Public Broadcasting System (PBS) telecasting. Clearly, for an actor, the LORT circuit is the plum of regional theatre activities. The best work of these theatres, while appealing primarily to their local audience, is regularly reviewed in trade papers, scholarly journals, and occasionally in *Newsweek, Time*, and the *New York Times*. An annual Tony Award gives further national prominence to the most outstanding LORT companies.

LORT theatres experienced a huge growth in the 70s and 80s; their numbers have pretty much leveled off since, however, perhaps due in some measure to declining financial support from the national endowments. But while LORT has stayed steady, giant steps by the so-called developing theatres, operating under Equity's Small Professional Theatre (SPT) and Letter of Agreement (LOA) contracts, have continued regional theatre's advance. By 1996 these developing theatres, which had employed fewer than a quarter as many actors as LORT ten years ago, employed nearly as many. Small Professional Theatres, often in small towns, may have ambitious agendas and offer outstanding artistic opportunities: A sampling of SPTs includes the Artists Repertory Theatre and Portland Repertory Theatre in Portland (Oregon), the Bathhouse Theatre in Seattle, the BoarsHead Theatre in Lansing (Michigan), the Borderlands Theatre in Tucson, the Purple Rose Theatre in Chelsea (Michigan), the Unicorn Theatre in Kansas City, and the theatre known as Thick Description in San Francisco.

Other nonprofit theatres in the TCG circuit also offer regular employment for actors, and sometimes even better break-in opportunities for acting aspirants. CATs (Chicago Area Theatres) are smaller-than-LORT companies in Chicago, including the superb Steppenwolf Theatre. HATs and BATs are Hollywood Area and (San Francisco) Bay area theatres respectively, and there's a BAPP rider (Bay Area Project Policy) for some experimental groups in the San Francisco region. Still more professional theatres—those with academic ties—may operate under University/Resident Theatre Association (U/RTA) contracts, as does the Pacific Conservatory of Performing Arts at Allen Hancock College. Other contracts—Guest Artist, Theatre for Young Audience (TYA), and Special Contract—may apply to these nonprofit groups.

Two other contracts exist for stock companies, which may be either commercial or nonprofit. Stock companies are organized under the Equity CORST or COST contracts (CORST = Council of Resident Stock Theatres; COST = Council of Stock Theatres) and present plays for stock runs (usually one or more weeks, and usually in the summer only, although some go year-round). CORST theatres must have a resident company of at least seven Equity members; many CORST theatres have apprentice programs and offer some possibilities for local actors (called "local jobbers") as well. COST theatres need have no stable company and in fact frequently produce prepackaged shows that simply bus from one COST theatre to another each week. Weekly stock—particularly at the New England summer theatres that once formed a "straw hat circuit"—used to be the great break-in venue for acting aspirants. This is where Mickey Rooney and Judy Garland found an old barn and said, "Hey, let's put on a play." But summer stock has now been relatively eclipsed as a professional starting place by the more intense LORT and even SPT resident movements.

Dinner theatres, which burst upon the American theatre scene in the early 1970s, have fallen back somewhat since then, but have now stabilized in number (currently at about one-third of the mid-70s high), providing another 21,000 professional actor work weeks on the dinner theatre contract. The theatrical fare at these houses consists, in the main, of light comedies and musicals; the plays are combined not only with pretheatre dinners, but occasionally posttheatre dancing and merriment, comprising a fairly encompassing entertainment medium. Some dinner theatres are beginning to offer apprentice programs, and apprentices who elect to serve as waiters and waitresses can make up to $500 per week while training. Occasionally dinner theatres offer year-round employment, which is a godsend to most actors; conversely the dinner theatre credit is not always a particularly helpful stepping stone to "eatless" ventures.

And there are some non-Equity companies—some employing Equity Guest Artists—in the regions too, which form sort of a fringe to the professional theatre. Shakespeare Festivals, now generally featuring more modern fare in addition to the namesake Bard, and outdoor drama festivals, featuring pageants of American history, are major groups of summer theatre companies, offering a range from well-paying to low-paying to no-paying opportunities in many states around the country. There are literally dozens of Shakespeare Festivals, including important ones in Oregon, Utah, Colorado, Texas, New Jersey, Vermont, Connecticut, California, Alabama, New York, Illinois, Idaho, among others. Most have at least some professional actors in key roles, but all audition nonprofessionals, at least for smaller parts. Summer theatre directories, such as that published by Jill Charles, list addresses and the audition dates for most of them. Many of the non-Shakespearean outdoor theatres are associated in an Institute of Outdoor Drama, headquartered at the University of North Carolina (see the appendix), which conducts annual unified auditions for many of its members.

Virtually all regional theatres are permitted to cast at least some of their season's roles with nonunion actors—and they do so regularly. Regional companies may also offer you a *direct* opportunity to break into the field, in that you can normally apply to audition directly to the theatre company, and need not be submitted by an agent. And, once on board in a regional theatre, you may then be able to work your way up to a union (Equity) card—if the theatre participates in the union's Equity Membership Candidate Program, as most LORT and Equity stock and dinner companies—and several SPT, CAT, and LOA companies as well—do. Under the *Equity Membership Candidate Program,* fifty weeks of acting work in one or more participating Equity companies can propel you into union membership. There's further information about this program in the "Unions" section of this chapter.

Overall, regional theatre (both profit and nonprofit) has become America's primary break-in place for actors, and it remains a significant employment area for American stage actors, even for Broadway veterans. Films and television also draw from regional banks. Casting director Mike Fenton reports that regional theatre is the source of 60% of the "unknowns" in Hollywood. And the number of regional plays that make their way to New York, with the same casts, is growing rapidly. Such Steppenwolf regulars as John Malkovich, Joan Allen, Glenne Headly, and Gary Sinise developed wonderful national reputations from their Chicago-based works.

But you must not assume that there is an automatic communication network among these theatres. Regional theatre remains in the regions, and credits there, however respectable, do not automatically turn into stepping stones to Broadway or Hollywood—if that's where you think you're headed. Regional credits may not even serve as stepping stones to other regional theatres, and actors employed at some of America's more remote companies, such as the Oregon Shakespeare Festival at Ashland, often find it difficult to audition for future jobs elsewhere while toiling away in the shadow of the Siskiyou Mountains. At Ashland and similar theatres, actors have created "shares" programs, at their own expense, flying in various LORT artistic directors to audition company members for future work at other theatres. To work in the regional theatre ("the provinces," they would say in England) is to develop a primarily local reputation, not a national one, and if you then plan to head for New York or Los Angeles, you had still better plan to start at the bottom when you get there (albeit with some valuable credentials).

Some actors, of course, have no wish to "go Hollywood" or to head for the Great White Way in the East. Hundreds of actors all over the country delightedly spend their entire careers in regional theatre, finding there a high degree of artistic fulfillment *and* social satisfaction. The Tony Award–winning South Coast Repertory Company in Costa Mesa, California, has maintained a core professional acting company (Don Took, Ron Boussom, Martha McFarland, Richard Doyle, Art Koustic, Hal Landon) for more than thirty years, thus proving that regular (if perhaps unspectacular) acting employment *does* still exist in the American theatre. But most actors eventually get frustrated after a decade or so in the regional circuits. Rene Auberjonois, a superb regional actor who "went on" to Broadway and Hollywood success, gives these reasons for leaving LORT: "Most actors in regional theatre are schizophrenics; they cannot reconcile the feeling that they should be fighting the fight of commercial theatre with the feeling that they are chosen members of some great and holy theatrical crusade. This dilemma gives rise to a working climate which could be compared to a monastery filled with self-consciously zealous monks suppressing the desire to ravage the neighboring village." It is evident that some of this "schizophrenia" is felt, if not to the same degree, by many in the LORT and other-lettered circuits.

## Getting into a Regional Theatre

Getting an acting job at a regional theatre is no easy task for a non-professional, but you probably have a better chance of getting your proverbial foot in the door—and even an audition—at a regional stage close to home than anywhere else in the acting business. While the leading LORT theatres cast many (if not all) of their major roles from a pool of New York–based Equity actors (with regional directors often travelling to New York to do so), or from the pool of professional actors already well-known on the regional LORT circuit, or, naturally, from their own resident professional company if such exists, virtually all regional theatres also arrange to see new actors from time to time right at home. Thus "general auditions" are scheduled at most theatres on a periodic basis: sometimes monthly, as with many of the larger companies: sometimes semi-annually (for example, in the fall and spring), as is more common with mid-sized ones. Of course, you can also be auditioned at any time that it strikes the theatre's fancy to see you, though this requires some serious application on your part—and some serious need on theirs—in order to happen.

Remember, though: The opportunity to audition for a professional theatre is a privilege, not a right. It's not the way it is in college, where your tuition payment guaranteed you a chance to be seen and heard. The theatre staff aren't required to see you or hear you; they have to want to do it. But virtually all regional theatres will see local non-professional actors if they apply, look promising, and are willing to wait around for their shot. Theatre companies are normally happy to have access to good actors who live in the immediate area (it saves them travel stipends and housing costs) and who might be available on short notice (for emergency replacements). This is good for the theatre's bottom line, and it makes for good public relations as well. We're not talking lead roles here, of course, or even necessarily speaking ones, but foot-in-the-door opportunities for beginning actors.

So, write or call your local theatre and ask if and when the company has general auditions, or "generals." If you write, you can include
a photo and resume. If you call, be sure you reach the number of the
business office, not the box office. And don't ask for the casting director: Just direct your question to the first person who answers, who will
either answer or redirect your call. Most regional theatres get so many
inquiries on this matter, in fact, that they've put their answer on the
recorded menu: "For information on general auditions, press 3." So
press 3 and try to get an appointment to audition. Failing that, see
what the drop-in policy is, and be prepared to come as often as it takes
in order to audition. Don't be alarmed if you don't hear back right
away. In casting season, these theatres will be receiving up to a thousand audition requests *each week,* and few companies have the clerical
staff to handle this process with complete accuracy (or even politeness). Be patient, be cool, and be inspiring.

What should you prepare for a regional theatre audition—if you
get the chance? There will be much more information on this later in
the book, but most regional theatres like to see one or two pieces, perhaps one of them classical, lasting in total no more than four minutes.
They will provide you with more specific guidelines if they have them.
Of course, if you know the theatre's current repertoire, its upcoming
shows, its philosophy, and its personnel before you show up, you can
try to select your material accordingly—and you obviously should:
There's no sense auditioning with traditional Shakespeare in a theatre
solely dedicated to the avant-garde, or vice versa. You will probably
audition on a rehearsal stage, or on an actual theatre stage, and will
probably be seen by the company's casting director and/or possibly
the artistic director plus, on occasion, their associates and staffs. You
should bring a photo and resume with you, even if you've sent one
ahead, and be sure your address and phone number are correct.

What are your chances? Well, of course they're very small. But
they're not zero. You should understand the complexities involved. As
one artistic director writes, with great sensitivity,

> The best chance a nonunion performer has is to be, first of all, an
> outstanding actor, and secondly a local resident. Then we know
> he or she will be easily available and won't need much money to
> live on. The odds against the auditioner are, of course, incredibly
> high. We see a good many fine actors. We have a very good selec-
> tion to choose from: It's a buyer's market. What isn't widely
> known is that we often see fresh faces that we want very much to
> give jobs to. I can think of three actors right now that I would

dearly love to work with. But you already have actors who are just as good and who are already hardworking members of your ensemble; you're certainly not going to bump them out of their jobs to make room for the new face. We have to remember that auditioning is a process for discovering a few new actors for your company, not casting all your roles.

So understand the picture, and try to fit yourself into it one way or another.

## Out of Town Auditions—and the Lottery

Of course, you can audition for a LORT or SPT theatre outside of your hometown as well. Just write or call as you would a local theatre. Many actors head for those few regional cities—Seattle and Chicago are most prominent—that have a major concentration of professional theatres and try to audition for all of them. If you do, of course, it's wise to arrange for some auditions ahead of time and plan to stay for a while. If you get work, you may find you have a new home.

Many LORT theatres and SPT theatres also audition in New York, often at TCG headquarters or the Actors Equity Association Audition Center, and sometimes at rented studios. These auditions are usually for specific roles in productions, but occasionally New York generals are held as well. Information can be found in the New York trade papers. And some regional theatres audition in Los Angeles and Chicago as well. However, admission to these auditions—which are designed for Equity members—is not entirely assured for non-professionals. For the past decade, nonunion actors who had met certain qualifications—working as an actor for two paid weeks was one of them—were determined to be "Eligible Performers" and were thus guaranteed equal status with Equity members in professional auditions. But the Eligible Performer status is in the process of being phased out as this book appears (see box), in favor of a plan that offers nonunion actors a "separate" audition from the Equity one. How this works out is anybody's guess at this point. Check the listings to find out if you're eligible (even if not Eligible) to audition.

*The LORT Lottery* is an opportunity to apply—Equity members only at this time—for a general audition with several LORT companies at the same time. LORT Lotteries are now held, twice a year in New York, once a year each in Chicago and Los Angeles. But it's—as its name indicates —a lottery, and a particularly low-odds one: You (and several thousand others) apply for one of 400 two-minute preliminary audition slots

## "Eligible Performer" Status — Is Now Defunct!

The Eligible Performer (EP) Card, which since 1988 has allowed certain non-Equity actors access to what were previously Equity-only auditions, is being phased out as this book goes to press. This action was taken via a negotiated arrgreement—approved by the National Labor Relations Board (NLRB) on May 2, 1997—between LORT, Equity, and the League of American Theatres and Producers (i.e. Broadway producers).

Henceforth (and once again), therefore, certain auditions will be limited to Equity members. But not all of them. The Board stipulates that employers cannot use their Equity auditions as an "exclusive referral system." Thus, producers must create some sort of alternative auditions for non-Equity actors. "If, in the future, the Employers cease using other hiring sources and employ individuals solely through the Equity audition system . . . it would be necessary to reexamine the conclusions herein to make additional findings regarding whether nonmembers of the Union are being discriminated against," ruled the board.

Moreover, while the agreement provides that employers must hold Equity auditions before "agent-submitted" auditions (which may involve non-Equity actors), the NLRB also rules that employers may not exclude non-Equity members from the casting pool, saying that while "experience, skill, knowledge, and appropriate physical characteristics for a given role" may be considered as legitimate criteria for casting a play, Equity membership may not be.

How will this work out? No one really knows. "Employers are under no obligation to hire employees solely through Equity auditions," says the Board. But won't they? "Employers are free to schedule other non-Equity auditions at any time," says the Board. But will they? Clearly, this will be an unsettled area over the coming months and years.

---

held during a three-day period, judged by representatives of three LORT theatres. If you win a slot, and your preliminary audition is outstanding, you're then invited to a follow-up general audition with casting directors from a number of companies. Your application for the lottery must be made on a 3 × 5 card (name, address, home and service telephone number, and Social Security number), with an accompanying self-addressed stamped number 10 envelope, and mailed or hand-delivered to the Equity office in the lottery city of your choice. If you've auditioned in either of the last two LORT lotteries, you won't be considered. If your name is drawn, you're notified by letter; be sure to cancel if you can't make it. Your resulting audition can be a monologue or scene; if you bring a scene partner, only your photo and resume can be submitted.

## Regional Combined Auditions

Wouldn't it be wonderful to go to one single audition and be seen by hundreds of artistic directors from around the country? This happens in other countries. Graduates of the Finnish National Theatre School, for example, audition in Helsinki at the end of their course of instruction for all the stage directors in Finland, and 'at the end of the audition, every graduate has a job! (On the other hand, only one in several hundred applicants make it into the Theatre School.) The diversification of theatre in this country, and the proliferation of drama schools, have made such cross-country auditions impossible, although for years TCG did run such a national audition.

There are several major groups that continue to hold unified regional auditions, however, and these are of varying use to the actor seeking employment.

The University/Resident Theatre Association (U/RTA) holds auditions at selected locales throughout the United States for nominated college students, followed by three finalist auditions in the New York, Chicago, and Los Angeles areas. These are not, ordinarily, auditions for professional work, however. Most of the opportunities offered by U/RTA are for paid graduate assistantships and fellowships at university drama programs, some of which are associated with resident theatres. Therefore, most of the U/RTA offerings will involve your enrollment in a Ph.D. or M.F.A. program at the host campus. Still, you may simultaneously or subsequently become involved with a related professional theatre company, and the U/RTA has proven to be a useful, if indirect, route to professional employment. For this reason, U/RTA should be investigated by interested college seniors. Write directly to U/RTA headquarters (1540 Broadway, Suite 3704, New York, NY 10036) for details, and try to get a nomination from your drama department chairperson.

Several other unified auditions, listed below, are for a mix of summer theatres, special summer productions, and some year-round companies. If you're interested, you should write for applications to these auditioning groups in December or January, to get a March or April audition for a summer acting job. Always include a business-sized self-addressed stamped envelope (SASE) with your request, and be prepared to pay a small auditioning fee. Remember, audition spaces are limited, and you may not even make it in; apply early, and present the strongest possible application. The main regional auditioners (as of 1997):

* The *Institute of Outdoor Drama* (IOD), CB 3240, Nations Bank Plaza, University of North Carolina, Chapel Hill, NC 27599-3240 (919/962-1328). This is an association of historical pageants, performed (obviously) outdoors. The pay is often quite good. The IOD will see 200 preregistered applicants, who must be at least 18 and have theatrical training. If you get in, you will be seen by about sixteen theatre companies from seven states, including *The Lost Colony* at Manteo, North Carolina; *Young Abe Lincoln* at Lincoln City, Indiana; and *Tecumseh!* in Chillicothe, Ohio. Website: www.unc.edu/outdoor/index.htm/

* The *Southeastern Theatre Conference* (SETC) is also headquartered at a University of North Carolina campus; SETC's annual convention includes a group audition for about eighty theatre companies, both summer and year-round. Send your SASE to the SETC at P.O. Box 9868, Greensboro, NC 27429-0868. You will have to join the SETC to audition, but you can do that at the convention itself, and then participate in the other convention activities. Some recent participants have been the Heritage Repertory Theatre of Charlottesville, Virginia; the Great American People Show in Champaign, Illinois; and the Sweet Fanny Adams Theatre & Music Hall of Gatlinburg, Tennessee. There is a fee for auditioning, which includes your SETC membership and convention fee. Website: www.spyder.net/setc/

* *The New England Theatre Conference* (NETC), Northeastern University, Department of Theatre, 360 Huntington Avenue, Boston, MA 02115. The NETC sees about 800 actors for nearly sixty theatre companies. Your application will be screened first (only about half the applicants are admitted to the audition), and there is a small audition fee. Certain LORT internship programs also audition here as well; among the many companies attending have been the Dorset Theatre Festival, the Cape Cod Melody Tent, the Boothbay Dinner Theatre, the Shawnee Playhouse, the Virginia Stage Company, the Berkshire Playhouse, the Actor's Theatre of

Louisville, and the Nutmeg Summer Theatre, among others. Website: www.world.std.com/~netc/index.htm/

- *StrawHat Auditions* take place in Manhattan and are said to offer more than 500 acting positions; send for information to StrawHat, 1771 Post Road East, Westport, CT 06880. Your completed application must include two photo-resumes, which will be reprinted and distributed to the producers. These include more than thirty summer companies from around the country, generally among them the Dorset Playhouse, Goodspeed Opera House, Williamstown Summer Theatre, Great American Melodrama, Powerhouse Theatre, and *Utah!* (a splashy outdoor musical). If you survive the screening, you will have two minutes to do two pieces, one of which can be a song. Producers advise that two-thirds of the actors hired will need to sing, but if you can't sing at a professional level, "don't try to bluff" your way through a song; do two monologues instead. There is a fee (currently $48).

- *Unified Professional Theatre Auditions.* About thirty companies, largely in the Midwest and South: Write to them at 51 South Cooper, Memphis, TN 38104.

- *Midwest Theatre Auditions,* Conservatory of Theatre Arts, Webster University, 470 E. Lockwood, St. Louis, MO 63119-3194. About sixty companies are involved here.

- *Ohio Theatre Alliance,* 77 High Street, 2nd Fl., Columbus, OH 43215-6108. About thirty companies.

Many other states and areas have theatre associations that conduct regional auditions, often at a different location every year. You can find out more by contacting your state or regional theatre association.

## THE BIG TOWNS

Sooner or later, however, you're almost certainly going to think about heading off to New York or Los Angeles. These are the "big bigs," as we've said (and as you no doubt already know), and there aren't too many people who go into this business who don't harbor at least some ambition to measure their powers in these most celebrated arenas. But which one?

### How to Choose?

Which town is easiest to "break into"? Neither, of course, is remotely easy, and there is no simple answer to the question; there are hundreds of variable factors. Most actors eventually try them both. Beware of those who say that "New York is finished" or "L.A. is impossible." Both these cities are tough, of course, but both will be employing hundreds of new actors each year; *each* one is finished for some, impossible for others.

Of course, you should know something about the towns themselves. They are utterly unalike, and both take some getting used to. New York is incredibly gruff, loud, fast-paced, and volatile; its subways could toughen an angel. Rents are sky-high, and middling restaurants charge twice what they do in Cleveland or Spokane. Substance abuse is a sidewalk sport in this town, and crime is endemic. On the other hand —well, this is America's premiere city, and for most of us New York's problems are dwarfed by its sheer magnificence. It's our publishing, broadcasting, advertising, art, and finance capital, as well as our theatre capital, and even a marginal life in New York City provides a heady climate and a thrilling intensity for any committed theatre artist. It's shocking how many plays are *set* here. New York, for all its flagrant faults, is at the very pulse of American culture, and not to know New York is to remain apart, to some extent, from the soul of the American stage.

Los Angeles, by contrast, is barely a city at all, but rather a vast desert plain, alternately broken up by urban concentrations (Hollywood, "downtown," Century City, Beverly Hills, Westwood, Universal City) and residential pastures—all crisscrossed by freeways to nowhere and the world's most indifferent system of public transportation. There is little in the way of an "L.A. Scene," since the city is vastly spread out and decentralized, and the people are among the most privacy conscious on earth. The real action of L.A. takes place within private homes and gated studios, and over Pacific Bell telephones—most of which (it often seems) are located in automobiles. The cellular conversation between two cars on the freeway is L.A.'s classic connection.

But geography is probably not the crucial factor in this decision. The key question is: Which *medium* do you plan to act in, or at least to begin your career in?

Well-trained stage actors, classical actors, and musical theatre performers should *usually* head for New York, for that's where most professional stage shows and musicals are cast—virtually all on- and off-Broadway; most stock (COST and CORST) and dinner; much LORT, SPT, and LOA. Even top-flight L.A. theatres cast a good deal in New York, infuriating southern California stage actors no end.

Conversely, those whose primary focus is on film and television work—particularly actors whose on-camera looks and personalities, and naturalistic acting abilities, are more likely to be selling points than stage training and experience—should head for Hollywood, the land of TV studios and feature films, as well as countless ninety-nine-seat showcase theatres, where actors perform on stage so as to be cast in films.

So, if you're bigger than life, musical- or rep-oriented, and eminently stageworthy, head for the Big Apple. And if you're drop-dead gorgeous, personality plus, intimate and contemporary, head instead for the Big Orange.

But, naturally, most actors fall somewhere in between. Wouldn't it be wonderful to live in England, where classical theatre, commercial theatre, films, and television are all headquartered in the same city? Where should the American in-betweens go? On margin (and this is a difficult call), this author recommends New York: first, because it is easier to get seen there; second, because there's more you can do there without an agent; third, because you won't need a car; fourth, because minor New York stage credits are more important in Hollywood these days than minor Hollywood TV credits are in New York; and fifth, because New York is the central casting locus for the regional theatre circuit. New York is also the site of most commercial photography shoots, cruise ship bookings, industrial shows (musical extravaganzas produced by corporations for their employees or stockholders), and half of the country's network soap operas, all of which provide good income, and acting—or acting-related—show business experience.

Finally, New York is an easier place to connect with a real theatre scene. In New York, if you're an actor and reasonably outgoing, it won't take you long to feel part of the theatre family, even if you're unknown and employed. Theatre bars, theatre bookshops, theatre lobbies, cheap ethnic restaurants on Eighth Avenue, and the TKTS line in Duffy Square (this is where you buy half-price tickets to Broadway and off-Broadway shows) all abound with actors like yourself. L.A. has little in the way of a comparable scene. In New York, you walk or take the subway everywhere, elbow to elbow with humanity—and other actors; in Los Angeles you're in a car and you're by yourself. So if you can't decide between the towns, I'd say try New York first.

How good is New York if you want to act in film? Well, some of the best film actors today began their careers on the New York stage or in regional theatre cast in New York. These include, in no particular order, Sigourney Weaver, Marlon Brando, John Goodman, Annette Bening, Mercedes Ruehl, Warren Beatty, Michael Jeter, Kathy Bates, Scott Bakula, Jason Alexander, Demi Moore, Bebe Neuwirth, Stacy Keach, Robert Duvall, Daniel Travanti, Al Pacino, Frank Langella,

Meryl Streep, Barbra Streisand, Jane Alexander, Robert DeNiro, Robert Redford, Dustin Hoffman, and Richard Dreyfuss. Stage to film, and New York to L.A., is the classic route. As the late James Coco said, "Off-Broadway auditions for Broadway, which auditions for Hollywood." More than ever before, film and even television directors look for actors well versed in improvisation, in stage acting—yes, even in classical performance technique. There are, of course, many Hollywood directors who shy away from what they feel are "arty off-Broadway know-it-alls." But New York credits are an important plus in any L.A. actor's portfolio. So if you're undecided between the two, and aiming to make your first career moves in stage acting (although it might not necessarily work out that way), New York should be your destination.

If, on the other hand, you are charismatic only on camera, are extraordinarily beautiful, or are determined to be a film or television performer, we'll say it again: Go west.

# Chapter 4

# Establishing Yourself

You have moved, then, to your new city. The first thing you must do is to *establish* yourself. Obviously you need a place to stay, and rents in both New York and L.A. are quite expensive—New York extraordinarily so (not to mention the rental agency, or "fixture," commissions you will probably be hit up for as well). If possible, move in with a friend and give yourself a couple of weeks to look for a rent-stabilized apartment in a decent area; better yet, move to New York with a friend or two and share a place and the rent among you. Bring enough money to pay two months' rent in advance plus a deposit, plus two thousand dollars in reserve. (Why two thousand dollars? It's a good round sum, and you'll need some real breathing room. Any less and you'll be in a state of constant fiscal panic before the end of the first week. But if it's out of the question, well, go anyway.)

If you head for Los Angeles, you can expect to find a more reasonably priced place to stay. It will also be cleaner and nicer to come home to. The limitation of L.A. is that you absolutely must have a *car* in good running condition. This will eat up whatever you may save on rent. (A car is not only unnecessary in New York, the parking rates there will make it a real liability, so leave your Toyota in Toledo.)

Once you are settled, you can get to work. There will be many things you need. There is no particular order in which you should get them, but you should get them fast. These are:

- A dependable source of income
- A telephone and a telephone service
- Photos

- A resume of your training and experience
- Colleagues
- Up-to-date information

## A DEPENDABLE SOURCE OF INCOME

Obviously you need a source of income that you can count on. You can't pay your bills, eat, dress, or go out into the world without money. Moreover, you cannot afford to scrimp on professional expenses like photographs and classes. Perhaps you have regular income from home, or from your working (and indulgent) spouse, or from a friend. If so, you need not worry as long as your source continues to take care of you, though generally something is expected in return. If you aren't so lucky, you will have to get a job, and preferably one with flexible hours that pays well. In Hollywood, since most work and interviews take place in the daytime, an evening job is ideal. For this reason, most L.A. area waiters are unemployed actors: Table waiting is *the* job of choice for most Hollywood thesps. In New York the same is true, until you start to perform or work at night in off-off-Broadway, when a morning or grave-yard shift may be preferable. The back pages of *Back Stage* and other trades advertise openings for temporary secretaries, word processors, administrative assistants, guy/gal Fridays, receptionists, bilinguals, clerks, and typists: If you have computer skills, you can make a living in either town.

A salable office skill is particularly valuable—you might land a job in a theatre-related area, and you will start to get contacts while you work. Many young men and women (male secretaries are now commonplace in Hollywood and are becoming so in New York) have started in the office and ended up on stage. If you can, do something you can be proud of, something you feel is professional. Being a professional at something is good training for being a professional at acting. Stay away from porn movies and illicit activities that may beckon; they will make you feel bad about yourself, which isn't going to help your acting one bit.

## A TELEPHONE—AND ALL THAT FOLLOWS

You can't do anything in show business without a telephone; this is an industry that relies on instant communications every step of the way.

Moreover, you will need a telephone contact even when you're not at home. The basic package these days, therefore, is a telephone, plus a telephone service, plus a reliable answering machine or voicemail service. Then, when things start getting fast and furious, you can add a pager—and maybe a cellular phone as well. You might even get a computer when you get the money together. Here's what these things can do for you.

The telephone is your basic contact with the casting world. It's where you make all your outgoing calls and receive calls from people to whom you give your number. Order your phone the minute you get a New York or L.A. address. Get the "call waiting" feature too, which will permit the casting director to interrupt your Mom's call and tell you that you got the part. You will also need to have an answering machine or voicemail service on that line, to take messages when you're not home. Unless you plan to be home three or four times a day, be sure to get a machine or voicemail service that you can call into from other phones to retrieve your messages: You won't want to be out of touch for too long. A word of advice: Keep your outgoing message short, distinct, and professional. Time is money, and long "cute" welcoming messages aren't so endearing to people (agents, say) who may have to call dozens of people every fifteen minutes.

You don't want to give your home number out casually, however, as that may invite all sorts of nuisance calls (and worse). You might also want to get instant notification of certain calls that come in when you're out of the apartment or out of town. For these reasons, you will also want a telephone service number for your business calls—at least until you get an agent who will take over receiving them. The telephone service—and there are dozens of these in both L.A. and New York—will receive your calls (on your line or on the service's) and take your messages, via either a live operator or a recording device (some are live until five, and recorded at night). You can then call in for those messages or have them forwarded to another number (your home number, for example) or have the service beep your pager, if you have one, to let you know a message has arrived. Then, if you're super-wired, you can return the call on your cellular phone! "Actors who use beepers tend to work more than those that do not," one casting director reports, because particularly as regards extras or under-fives (parts with less than five lines), "there isn't a lot of time to wait for people to call back. I have to cast the show for the next day so production can do the preparation and paperwork." Cellular phones aren't quite so necessary—you can usually find a phone nearby—but they're certainly a convenience if you can afford one. The pager's advantage over a cell phone, in addition to being a lot cheaper, is that it's smaller, and you can keep it in your pocket all day long without the batteries running out. And if you want to protect your privacy, and sense of public decorum, you can even get one that—instead of beeping—just tickles your thigh a bit, thus not disturbing the people around you (who might be angling for the same part!).

Some telephone services are bicoastal or nationwide and can give you your own 800 number so you can receive toll-free messages from anywhere in the country. Starting prices for these services, with minimum bells and whistles, is around $5 per month; added services can up that figure considerably. Choose your service carefully; it's a high turnover business. If the service is computer-operated, make sure the machinery is reliable and free from static. If it has live operators, give them a few test calls and see how polite they are in answering the phone. Naturally, ask your friends—if you have any who already subscribe. Most entry-level actors have services, and list their service numbers, not their home numbers, on their resumes; it's business-like, and it protects your privacy. When you get an agent, however, you will list the agent's number.

A fax machine and a computer might be worthwhile additions to your communications network, if you can afford them. Faxes are first-rate for getting "sides" (partial scripts) at home prior to auditions: There are services that can fax them to you when you get cast. And e-mail—via computer—is becoming a useful tool for hooking up with a rapidly increasing number of individuals and offices in the acting industry. Connections to the Internet also offer you access to several on-line information and casting opportunities worldwide. The venerable *Players Directory*, which comes out three times a year in Los Angeles and provides photos and contact points for virtually all professional film and TV actors, is now available in CD-ROM as well as print editions. The electronic communication age is clearly here and is transforming the acting industry as you read this.

## PHOTOGRAPHS

Your photos are your calling cards; no actor can be without them. You may want them in as many as five different forms.

- Headshots. These are mass-produced black-and-white pictures, 8 × 10 inches (vertical), showing your head and shoulders.

Headshots are the most prevalent actor photographs in use today on both coasts and around the country.

- Three-quarter bodyshots, or "3/4 shots." These are also mass-produced 8 × 10 black-and-whites that you might use as alternates to headshots. Sometimes also called hip shots, they show you from the hips upward, giving a sense of your body as well as your face. Three-quarter shots have come into vogue in the late 90s; whether they stay in vogue is an open question at the time of writing. Many casting people like them, others loathe them. If your body is a strong selling point, you might consider a 3/4 shot as an alternate or even as your main photo—but the straight headshot remains standard, particularly in New York.

These are your *most important* photos, but you may also want:

- Composite photos, which combine head shots and perhaps 3/4 shots in a variety of expressions, make-ups, and costumes. Composites are rarely used today, however, and then almost exclusively for TV commercials. Entry-level actors will have little use for them unless they are headed strictly for the commercial market. Again, 8 × 10 and black and white.

- Photos for your "book," which you carry around to interviews and auditions to show interested casting people how you look in different costumes. Like the composite, however, the "book" is rarely used these days, and then almost exclusively in modeling and commercials. It might be nice to carry such a loose-leaf around, though, if it doesn't get in your way. And you never know who might want to see what you look like in a Stetson or bikini (or both). Black and white are standard, but color's acceptable: After all, it's *your* book.

- Postcard shots, which consist of your reduced headshot or 3/4 shot printed on a postcard stock that still leaves plenty of room for an address and message. These can be printed at the same time as your distribution photos, and you can use them for confirming dates, inviting people to showcases, and, in general, reminding casting folk who you are. Black and white shots are most common, but here, again, color can occasionally be used to effect.

You can, of course, acquire photos for all of these purposes at the same time. Find a photographer who specializes in actor photos (we'll talk about how you do that below) and arrange a sitting. In a few days (sooner if you pay for it) you will be shown one or more sets of contact sheets. Each set consists of thirty-six photos taken with a standard 35-

millimeter camera; if you've had a three-roll sitting, you'll have over a hundred photos to study. Pick your favorites (you might take them home to some friends for their advice) and have the best of them blown up to full 8 × 10 size. Then pick the best of *them*, and have your master shot—presumably your headshot—mass-produced for distribution. The rest will go into your book, if you have one.

Your photographer might charge as little as $100 (one in L.A. currently advertises an "emergency headshot" for $50), or the price might be as much as showbiz traffic will bear: The best-known New York and L.A. actor photographers can charge from $500 to well into the four figures for a session. The photographer's price normally includes, in addition to the shooting session, some blow-ups to examine for your final selection. You may have to pay extra for the negatives if you want them, though this is often negotiable. You may pay the photographer extra, too, for make-up and wardrobe services and/or for photo retouching, if the photographer arranges these extras (none of them, though, are necessary, or even a good idea).

You don't get your mass-distribution photos from the photographer, however; for this you will take your master shot to a photo lab or reproduction service. The lab will add your name (and, if you have an agent, the agency's logo) to the bottom of the photo, and print 8 × 10s by the hundred, using either a lithographic or photographic process. Lithos, which like photos can be reproduced in glossy, matte, or "pearl" finishes, are somewhat cheaper, generally running about $50 for a hundred, and as little as $99 for five hundred. Postcards are a bit less than this: Four hundred 6" × 4" postcards for $65 is a currently advertised price. If you want your photos on actual photographic paper, not lithographed, you will pay a bit more. These prices, by the way, aren't much more than they were twenty-five years ago: a rare blessing in this business.

It's easy to find photographers and photo reproduction services. There are dozens of advertisements for each in the trades in any given issue. There are many more listed and advertised in *The Working Actors Guide* and similar informational volumes published every year in L.A. and New York, and on the acting shelves of drama book shops in both cities (see the appendix). Finding *good* photographers, however, is a little more difficult. You'll have to get recommendations, study the ads and information you can glean, and look at their previous work.

This means, of course, you'll have to know what you want—which is no easy matter. Unfortunately, everybody has an idea—and often a different idea—about what constitutes a good actor photograph. And it seems everybody will hate yours. Don't be surprised when you get to

*Tyler Layton*

An appealing three-quarter shot of this young stage and television actress.

# Tyler Layton • *SAG*

**Gold Marshak Liedtke Associates**
Talent and Literary Agency

3500 West Olive Avenue Suite 1400
Burbank, California 91505

Eyes: Blue
Hair: Light Brown
Height 5'6"
Weight: 113

## Television

| | | |
|---|---|---|
| Silk Stalkings | Series Lead | USA Network |
| Brotherly Love | Guest Star | NBC |

## Theatre*

| | | |
|---|---|---|
| Noises Off | Brooke | Univ. of California, Irvine |
| Cat on a Hot Tin Roof | Maggie | Univ. of California, Irvine |
| As You Like It | Phebe | Univ. of California, Irvine |
| Shoemaker's Holiday | Rose | Utah Shakespeare Festival |
| As You Like It | Celia | Utah Shakespeare Festival |
| Bloody Poetry | Claire | Univ. of California, Irvine |
| Hedda Gabler | Thea | Univ. of California, Irvine |
| Fool for Love | May | Univ. of California, Irvine |
| The Bear | Popov | Univ. of California, Irvine |
| Olympe's Marriage | Pauline | Univ. of California, Irvine |
| Romeo and Juliet | Juliet | Black Warrior Shakespeare |
| Taming of the Shrew | Biondello | Porthouse Theatre |
| Miss Julie | Christine | AB Studio |
| What the Butler Saw | Geraldine | AB Studio |
| Fifth of July | Shirley | AB Studio |
| As You Like It | Audrey | Univ. of Alabama Mainstage |
| Our Town | Emily | Vestavia Hills Theatre |
| Quilters | Ensemble | Univ. of Alabama Mainstage |
| The Promise | Lika | Univ. of Alabama Mainstage |

* Partial list from 40 plays

**Commercials & Industrials** (Lists Upon Request)

## Training

Master of Fine Arts, Drama-University of California, Irvine 1996
Bachelor of Fine Arts, Drama-University of Alabama 1990
**Acting:** Univ. of California, Irvine: Robert Cohen, Eli Simon, Martha McFarland, Keith Fowler
University of Alabama: Jonathan Michaelsen & John Hardy
Kent State University: Kate Ingram
**On-Camera Acting:** Eric Klein (Univ. of California, Irvine)
**Voice:** Univ. of California, Irvine: Dudley Knight & Joan Melton
University of Alabama: Stewart Vaughn & Alan Bales
Kent State University: Christine Adaire
**Combat:** Chris Villa (Univ. of California, Irvine)
**Movement:** Annie Loui (Univ. of California, Irvine)

Can do all kinds of Southern Accents • Dialects • Swimming • Stage Combat •
Painting • Running • Softball • Can sing (a little)

New York or Hollywood and the people there tell you that the photos you've brought with you from home are horrible. Of course, they might *be* horrible, particularly if they were taken by your little sister who is an amateur photographer, or even by your hometown photo studio pro. Actor photos are a specialized commodity, and in New York and Hollywood they are common currency—whole restaurant interiors are covered with them. Everybody in those towns, it seems, considers him or herself an expert on what your photos—and you—should look like. Plus, lots of people in town know a photographer of their own—maybe it's *their* little sister—who, they will say, can "do you" better. There's also going to be a current trend in photos for the year, or even the month, you arrive in town: maybe brushstroke borders, or cockeyed angles, or 3 × 3 square pictures floating in 8 × 10 white. Basically, judging photos is a notoriously subjective subject and can be especially painful when *you're* the subject. You're going to have some decisions to make, both in choosing a photographer and specifying what you want. Here are a few things you should look for and ask for, judging by a survey of casting directors.

Above all, *yes, absolutely above all,* your photos must look like you. And you must look like your photos, which is not exactly the same thing, since your looks will change while your photos won't: If you no longer look like your old 8 × 10, get a new one. Every casting director and agent in the world, when asked what they're looking for in a photo, will start off by saying they want it to look just like you; moreover, they'll get in a rage if they call you in on the basis of the photo and you show up looking like something (or somebody) else. So, throw out those old photos, plus the retouched glamour shots, if you please.

If there's another common line that CDs recite about photographs, it's that the best pictures show both life and warmth. "Someone approachable, someone you wouldn't be afraid to speak to," says Sheila Manning of Jeff Greenberg Casting, who looks at hundreds of photos ("200 in a minute and a half") every day to cast both TV shows and commercials. Manning hates tricky formats, forced smiles, shticky hands-on-face shots, composites ("It shows me it's old, and from what she is wearing, she's out of date"), and "anything that looks phony." Her views are mainstream. Another casting director seeks "life behind the eyes—something going on that tells you about who the person is, as opposed to a flat, pretty picture." Another likes photos that show "life going on in their face, intelligence in their eyes, as opposed to a vapid look of, 'Aren't I cute?' 'Aren't I pretty?'"

So naturalness, liveliness, and a sense of excitement are the crucial elements of great photos, and are much more important than clever poses and splashy formats. The rapport you can develop with your photographer, then, becomes particularly important, so that your mind and emotions can become fully engaged during your shoot and your natural liveliness can come out. Thus it's not only important to see a photographer's work, but also to get a good sense of the photographer's personality and working methods. You certainly don't want to be intimidated or brushed off by your photographer, no matter how celebrated. Shooting location may also play a role: Outdoor shots, with natural lighting, can convey warmth and genuineness—but they can also make you squint from the sunlight, or get lost in the busy-ness of background. Studio shots give you more control—your hair won't blow around, for example—but can look more, well, studious. If you shoot outdoors, be sure the photographer can blur out the background— which is easily done by setting the proper focal length. If you shoot in a studio, be sure you feel at home there.

What should you wear for your shoot? You should discuss this in advance with the photographer and arrange for a selection of two or three outfits. Natural, contemporary, relaxed clothing you feel good in, and that brings out the "inner you," will always be best. Avoid bold patterns such as stripes or plaids, anything that's uncomfortable, anything that's super-trendy (for, among other things, it will quickly date). Photographer Ike Eiseman suggests that clothing that has a physical texture—such as "tweed jackets, sweaters, denims"—looks particularly good. Clothing, though casual, should be spotless, hair clean, jewelry and make-up discreet (if used at all), and eyes open and shining.

Should you smile? The answer is a definite "yes" for commercials and daytime TV—at least if you have good teeth. The smile has to be genuine and infectious, however. A relaxed photo session will help this come out. Theatrical pictures can be more sober and serious, to be sure, but frowns and glowers are probably best avoided.

When you get your contact sheet, look at your pictures very carefully; you should use a magnifier to see them in detail. Disregard photos in which your eyes are anything but brilliant, or that have distracting backgrounds (or foregrounds), or that show smudges on your clothing, or that present your face in less than perfect focus. Show the contacts to your friends and to people in the business, and get their opinions—taking the proverbial grain of salt as you do.

And ask the photographer—who will undoubtedly offer advice in any event. If none of the shots please you, ask for a reshoot; it may be a sticky request, but they're your photos, and it's your career. On the other hand, if you've got a good photographer, consider his or her

BRIAN
THOMPSON

Basic headshot and resume of West Coast–based actor, Brian Thompson, in the second decade of his career.

Agent:
Gold/Marshak & Associates

Manager:
Daniel Doty

# Brian Thompson

**FILM** (partial listing)

| | |
|---|---|
| DRAGONHEART | UNIVERSAL/Rob Cohen |
| STAR TREK VII | PARAMOUNT/Rick Berman |
| TED & VENUS | COLUMBIA/Bud Cort |
| LIFE STINKS | PARAMOUNT/Mel Brooks |
| PASS THE AMMO | VISTA/David Beaird |
| THE NAKED TRUTH | OMEGA/Nico Mastorakis |
| COBRA | WARNER BROTHERS/George Cosmotis |
| MOON 44 | CENTROPOLIS/Roland Emmerich |
| THREE FUGITIVES | DISNEY/Francis Veber |
| LYONHEART | UNIVERSAL/Sheldon Lettich |
| HIRED TO KILL | INHAUS PICTURES/Peter Rader |
| MIRACLE MILE | TRI-STAR/Steve DeJarnett |
| YOU TALKIN' TO ME | UA/Irwin Winkler |
| FRIGHT NIGHT II | VISTA/Tommy Lee Wallace |
| ALIEN NATION | FOX/Gale Anne Hurd |
| TERMINATOR | ORION/Jim Cameron |
| IN THE COLD OF THE NIGHT | OMEGA/Nico Mastorakis |
| THREE AMIGOS | ORION/John Landis |

**SERIES/PILOTS**

| | |
|---|---|
| KINDRED | FOX/Peter Medak |
| KEY WEST | FOX/David Beaird |
| THE OWL | CBS/Tom Holland |
| WEREWOLF | FOX/John Ashley, Frank Lupo |
| CONAN THE LIBRARIAN | PBS/Larry & Cecily Lancit |

**EPISODIC** (partial listing)

| | |
|---|---|
| X-FILES | FOX/Rob Bowman |
| THE ADVENTURES OF HERCULES | SYND/Sam Raimi |
| DEEP SPACE NINE | SYND/David Livingston |
| SOMETHING'S OUT THERE | NBC/Richard Colla |
| GEORGE BURNS COMEDY SHOW | UNIVERSAL/Phil Alden Robinson |

**THEATRE** (partial listing)

| | |
|---|---|
| MACBETH | Colorado Shakespeare Festival |
| THE KING & I | Riverside Civic Light Opera |
| OLIVER | TOP Theatre |
| BITTERSWEET | Longbeach Civic Light Opera |
| TERRA NOVA | University of California, Irvine |
| OEDIPUS | University of California, Irvine |

**Skills:** Martial Arts, Weapons, Broadsword, Foil, Sabre, Horses, Piano, Guitar, Sushi Rolling.

**Training:** Master of Fine Arts in Acting, University of California, Irvine
**Acting:** Edward Albee, Jerzy Grotowski, Bob Cohen, Bill Needles (Stratford, Canada), Brewster Mason (Stratford, England).
**Dialects & Speech:** Dudley Knight, Carla Meyer
**Voice:** Joan Zajec, Seth Riggs

BRIAN THOMPSON

Professional character shots of Thompson submitted for specific auditions.

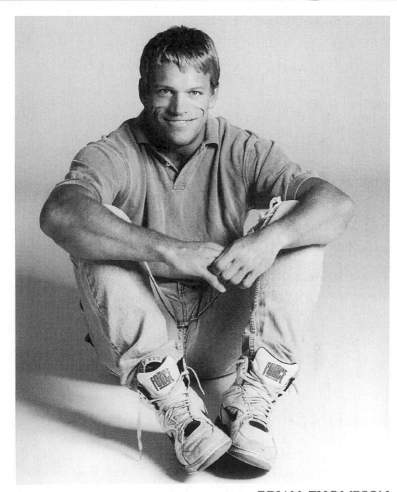

BRIAN THOMPSON

advice carefully. The photographer wants your pictures to be successful too; it's essential for his or her business—as well as yours.

## TAKING YOUR OWN PHOTOS?

You may, of course, want to take your own photographs; photography is not, after all, a very mysterious art. Perhaps you feel you have photographic talent, or maybe you haven't been able to find a good photographer, or maybe you just can't afford the going price for a sitting. Why not give it a try? Get a friend, a good camera and a telephoto lens (you can rent these for a day), and take a few rolls of black and white film down to the local park. If you come up with some good pictures, have them professionally processed and enlarged at a camera shop. Some actors even shoot themselves with a time-release button on the camera. Now, *most* homemade photos of this variety are pretty useless, because a fine photo involves careful attention to lighting, pose, background, angle, and composition, but if you are exceptionally talented and/or lucky, you might manage a classy, bright, intriguing picture. But don't settle for less. If you end up with nothing but a roll of snapshots, swallow your pride, dig into your wallet, and go to a pro. After all, you're about to become one yourself, aren't you?

## DEMO REELS

It's common now for TV and film actors—particularly in the L.A. market—to have, in addition to their still photos, a "demo reel" (or "film on yourself") showing the actor in actual performance. This is not for beginners: Demo reels (also called demo tapes) are almost always a collection of *professional* credits—clips from your best film and TV roles that have been professionally edited into a winsome, compelling, five- to seven-minute videocassette presentation. The demo reel is not a documentation of your career, just a quick montage of your acting skills. It should be varied, appealing, and, let me repeat, professional above all; this is not a time to gather up home videotape of your college performances or student film experiments. Still, particularly if you head to L.A., you'll be up against such reels right off the bat, so you should know about them now—and be getting into position to make your own.

When you do start to get professional film and TV credits, you should do everything you can to acquire broadcast-quality tapes (3/4

**TANGI MILLER**

A headshot—verging toward three-quarters—of a student actress at the start of her professional career.

inch, Super VHS, or Beta-SP) of them. If you can only get 1/2 inch VHS off the air (which you can record yourself with a VCR), at least record it in SP mode. When on the set, you can help yourself out enormously by making a friend of the show's production coordinator, and asking—at an appropriate moment, of course—for a copy of all the raw footage (tape or film) that includes you, including master shots, close-ups, two-shots, and, of course, a copy of the final project. This means that if you've got some good stuff that lands on the cutting room floor, it can still be included in your demo. You might offer to provide the 3/4 inch tape for your own copy to make this easier. Lacking an in-house tape of your performance, you can also arrange with a video editing service, which you'll be hiring to edit your tape (see below) anyway, to tape your TV clip onto broadcast-quality tape right off the air. You need to arrange this sufficiently ahead of time. Some video services may even have you on their backlog tape file, which several maintain.

When you've accumulated four or five suitable clips, from whatever source(s), you can find any of a number of video editing and duplication services that will produce your reel: converting film to tape (where necessary), editing your clips (with straight cuts, or with any special wipes or dissolves or freeze frames you may want), putting in your titles and your headshot, and making your dubs (copies) on regular VHS (1/2 inch) videocassettes—which you can then pop into any casting office VCR, or mail out when the situation presents itself. The minimum cost for this will likely be about $125—for a single title card and straight editing cuts—to about double that for such effects as digital ("toaster") editing, wipes and dissolves between clips, flips and tumbles (not advised!), multiple title cards, a complete montage with music, and photos (for example, your headshot) downloaded to tape. Once you've got a usable master demo, you make dubs for a nominal charge: about five dollars—plus the cost of the tape—per copy. The current issue of *The Working Actors Guide* or the Hollywood yellow pages is a good source of ads for video studios specializing in this; most will be happy to show you some sample reels.

Demo-reel advice from the pros: Keep it short—six minutes maximum, and four is better. Keep your titles and video effects simple and classy; you, not the editor, must be the star. Keep your character relatively consistent: Vary the moods and tempos, but not your basic image; don't try to be a one-person repertory company. Finally, if any of your outtake video clips include a time code at the bottom (which is the running digital clock used in editing the final version), leave it *on*: it subliminally validates the clip's (and your) professionalism.

Of course, you can also make a demo yourself, which many of the video services will be happy to help you with, providing a studio and whatever else you might need: a director, camera operators, sound mixers, engineers, and other technicians, as well as editing and duplication. You can even do this "on location" if you wish. Costs, you should realize, are relatively high, and effectiveness is probably way low: Many casting people consider these as simply homemade vanity reels. If you can do something truly fantastic on tape, however, this might be one way to get it across.

## RESUMES

Your resume is a listing of the parts you have played (and where, and—if impressive—with whom), printed on a single sheet, together with some basic information: your name; your service number (or, if you have an agent, your agent's number); your height, weight, hair and eye color; and your union affiliation, if any. Union affiliation is so important it should go right under your name, the magic letters being AEA, SAG, AFTRA.

There are also some occasional oddities you might mention at the bottom if you think they might be helpful in getting you work: who you trained with, what specialties you can do. "Tape available on request" announces you have a demo reel (see above). The resume is then stapled to the back of your photograph. Some photo labs can actually print your resume on the back of your photo, but that's not, in fact, a very good idea. Your resume will need to be updated regularly (you hope!) and you won't want to have new photos printed each time.

Your resume should be carefully composed, professionally typed, and cleanly printed. While no actor ever got hired because of an expensive printing job on a photo-resume, and while superopulence can be an actual turn-off, *neatness* and *clarity* are very important; they indicate your professionalism.

There is no single format, but there are some general parameters you should stay within.

What information should you list on a resume? As to your physical characteristics, be honest. List your real—not your ideal—height and weight, or casting people will be mad when you turn out fatter or shorter than you led them to expect. Keep the description of your hair color up to date, if you go in for makeovers in that area. If you sing, give your vocal range. You don't need to list an age or an age range;

## Jennifer Roszell

Headshot and resume of New York–based stage and daytime television actress Jennifer Roszell.

# DULCINA EISEN ASSOCIATES

## JENNIFER ROSZELL
### AEA - SAG - AFTRA

Height 5'7"
Weight: 120
Hair: Brown
Eyes: Brown
Voice: Soprano

**Television**

| | | |
|---|---|---|
| GUIDING LIGHT | Eleni Andros Cooper (currently on contract) | CBS |

**Regional Theatre**

| | | | |
|---|---|---|---|
| THE SCHOOL FOR WIVES | Agnes | Victoria Bussert | Great Lakes Theatre Festival |
| THE KING STAG | Angela | Andrei Belgrader | American Conservatory Theatre |
| OUR COUNTRY'S GOOD | Mary Brenham/Rev'd | Beth Craven | Clarence Brown Theatre |
| MAN AND SUPERMAN | Ann Whitefield | Tom Cooke | Clarence Brown Theatre |
| OTHER PEOPLE'S MONEY | Kate Sullivan | John Eisener | The Colonial Theatre |
| WHEN WE DEAD AWAKEN | Lady | Robert Wilson | American Repertory Theatre |
| SERVANT OF TWO MASTERS | Clarice | Andrei Belgrader | American Repertory Theatre |
| MEDIA AMOK (Chris Durang) | Mary Lou Popper | Les Waters | American Repertory Theatre |
| THE ISLAND OF ANYPLACE | Great Grandfooler | Thomas Derrah | American Repertory Theatre |
| HAMLET | Ophelia (u/s) | Ron Daniels | American Repertory Theatre |
| I'M NOT RAPPAPORT | Laurie | David Ira Goldstein | Arizona Theatre Company |
| OEDIPUS | Oedipus | Const. Arvanitakis | Arizona Theatre Company |

**New York**

| | | | |
|---|---|---|---|
| THE STORYTELLER | The Aunt | Seth Donsky | Manhattan Theatre Club (in house) |
| "WHATTAYA BLIND?"(Musical Review) | Various | Ike Schambelan | Theatre by the Blind @ J. Anderson |

**American Repertory Theatre Institute (selected)**

| | | |
|---|---|---|
| FEAR AND MISERY | | |
| OF THE THIRD REICH* | The Wife, etc. | Ron Daniels |
| ORESTES | Helen | Tina Landau |
| KASIMIR & KAROLINE | Karoline | Allan Zadoff |
| GOOD PERSON OF SETZUAN | God #1, The Wife | Beth Milles |
| THE VAGABOND | The Wayfarer | Spenser/Colton |

*also performed at International Theatreschool Festival in Amsterdam

**Commercials**
(Conflicts upon request)

**Voiceover**

| | | | |
|---|---|---|---|
| THE MARK OF THE | | | |
| MUSKETEERS (cartoon) | Constance (principal) | Tug Yourgrau | The Monitor Channel, WQTV |

**Training**
American Repetory Theatre Institute for Advanced Theatre Training, Harvard University
University of California, Irvine - Bachelor of Arts

| | |
|---|---|
| **Acting:** | Robert Cohen, Ron Daniels, Thomas Derrah, Alvin Epstein, Christine Estabrook, Keith Fowler, Jeremy Geidt, Jerzy Grotowski, William Needles, Jane Nichols |
| **Voice:** | Bonnie Raphael, Dudley Knight |
| **Singing:** | Annette Masson, Mehlon Schanzenbach, Adrienne Angel |
| **Voiceover:** | Stuart Dillon |
| **Movement/Dance:** | Jessica Sayre, Amy Spencer, Richard Colton, Bill Irwin (workshop) |
| **Special Skills:** | Dialects (list upon request), Dance (jazz, tap, ballroom), Mime, Mask, Stage Combat |

### 154 East 61st Street        New York City 10021

your photo should show that adequately. Most casting directors feel that giving your age limits you more than it helps you. *If you are under 18,* however, give your *birth date,* as there are legal restrictions on your hiring that the casting people will need to know about beforehand. After 18, make new resumes.

As to your credits, your professional experiences are *by far* the most important ones. If you are in L.A., looking for film/TV work, then list film/TV work first; if you are looking for stage opportunities, head your resume with those. If you have acted with any union company, that credit should be listed above your amateur ones, even if the work was artistically inconsequential—if you have been an extra on a TV pilot, for example, put it above the Hamlet or Hedda you did in college. If you have acted with known stars, known directors, known actors, or known theatre companies, choose a format that highlights this information. Your resume is not a passive document, an application form to be faithfully filled out: It is a creative statement, an advertisement of your skills. Don't approach it as a duty but as art: a creative opportunity. If your experience is limited solely to college or school shows, list them proudly, and make them seem as if they were the most important shows done in the three-state area where you lived.

But don't lie! Aside from moral reasons, you'll probably get caught. It's really a small world out there, and people do check. If you say you've acted for Peter Brook, the director who's interested in you might very well *call* Peter Brook to check you out; and if you really haven't, then you're in the muck. Or the person in the back of the room might *be* Peter Brook; you never can tell.

Want another reason not to lie? You'll be worrying the whole time that you'll be found out, and it will spoil your audition. Furtiveness and anxiety are disastrous for actors on an interview, and you only set yourself up for a sour stomach if you know you are presenting forged credentials.

At the bottom of your resume, you can include some miscellaneous information:

- Your special abilities (for example, performance sports, such as high diving or gymnastics, which you do superbly; circus acts; singing and dance experience; fencing skill; nightclub work; and so on)
- Your training in acting, singing, dance (listing the names of your instructors if they are well known outside your school)
- Languages you speak fluently, and dialects you can do fluently

Keep this "bottom" material to less than 10% of the resume.

You should *not* include the following kinds of information on your resume:

- Your interest or experience in directing or stage managing (it can be a turn off)
- Your membership in Phi Beta Kappa (ditto: "It doesn't do to be too smart. Actors who insist that they're brilliant—that puts you out of the running for half the roles you want to play," says Edward Herrmann)
- Your high school or college grades (nobody cares)
- Your hobbies (ditto)
- Your reasons for wanting a job (they know)
- Your dedication to acting (they know that too)
- Your willingness to do anything and everything (they'll find that out later if they cast you)
- Your psychological history (ditto)
- Your marital situation (it may change)

How cute should you be? Watch it. If you want to include a couple of humanizing details (such as your astrological sign or your ownership of wire-haired terriers), you might spark a conversation in an interview, but more likely you'll simply come off as an amateur. It's best to be simple, honest, effective, and businesslike, showing your experience at a glance.

Don't pad your resume. You can't make up for a lack of quality in your credits by substituting quantity. Actors who cram thirty-five amateur roles onto one sheet of paper only make it clear that they have been wasting away in the boondocks longer than has been good for them. It is better to show a half-dozen credits that look interesting than five dozen that look repetitious.

## UNIONS

Your union affiliation, we have said, goes at the top of the resume. That may strike a note of terror in your mind—for how do you get into the union? You are probably already aware of the great "cycle of impossibility" that defines union membership: You can't get work until you are a member of the union, and you can't be a member of the union until you get work. Well, that's not true anymore, not exactly. (It never was true, of course, it only *seemed* true.) You can get into the unions now somewhat more easily than in years back, but then union membership may not mean quite so much as it did then.

You have to understand, at the outset, that it's the *job* of unions to keep you out. That's one of the main reasons why there *are* unions: to keep you out of the picture (literally and figuratively). Unions protect their existing members, to whom you represent a threat—and, to be brutally frank, a cheap threat.

Remember, though, you will come to be happy there are unions. They will protect *you* if you become an actor. And if there were no actors' unions, actors wouldn't get minimum salaries, wouldn't get health benefits, wouldn't get fair working conditions, and wouldn't have retirement plans. Do you really think theatre owners would come up with retirement programs for actors on their own initiative? No, theatre owners have their hands full planning next year's season. The unions take care of the actors' long-range welfare. So the unions aren't the enemy, even though they may seem lined up against you at the beginning.

As I write this, there are three principal actors' unions, already referred to in these pages. The Actors' Equity Association (AEA, commonly called Equity), with its 33,000 members, is the union for all professional stage actors; it's the oldest performer's union in America, founded in 1913, and has its main headquarters in New York, with branches in Los Angeles, Chicago, Orlando, and San Francisco. Professional actors working in film and TV are, at the time of writing, unionized by either the 84,000-member Screen Actors Guild (SAG), for film and filmed television, or the 70,000-member American Federation of Television and Radio Artists (AFTRA), for videotaped TV—including most soap opera performers as well as sportscasters, game show hosts, political commentators, and program announcers. SAG is a national union, with headquarters in Los Angeles and branches around the country; AFTRA is a more loosely amalgamated federation of local unions. By the time you read this, however, SAG and AFTRA will most likely have merged into a single union, since a merger blueprint was approved in 1994, and a comprehensive constitution for a merged union—still unnamed—was approved in November 1996. Actual implementation of a SAG–AFTRA successor union could be expected by late 1997 or early 1998.

As many professional actors belong to more than one of these unions, and as many now-AFTRA members are not actors, you cannot simply add up the membership totals of each to determine the number of professional actors in the United States, but 120,000 is a reasonably good estimate as to this country's unionized acting pool.

The three principal actor unions are joined by the American Guild of Variety Artists (AGVA) and the American Guild of Musical Artists (AGMA) in a loose association known as the Associated Actors and Artists of America (the Four "A's"). All these unions and guilds operate under American Federation of Labor–Congress of Industrial Organizations (AFL–CIO) charters, and SAG, particularly, emphasizes its AFL–CIO constituent status to achieve greater political clout than it could achieve on its own.

How can *you* join a union? Method one, the cleanest and most effective way by far if you can swing it, is simply to be offered an acting job by a union producer—that is, by a producer willing to sign you to a union contract. In that happy event, the union will be obligated to let you in, subject only to your paying a hefty initiation fee ($800 for Equity, $800 for AFTRA, $1,080 for SAG), plus a first installment on your semiannual dues (which are dependent on your salary, but at minimum, currently, $39 for Equity, $42.50 for SAG and AFTRA). Note that you don't always *have* to join the union just because you have a union job. A provision of the Taft–Hartley Act permits you to work in a union production for up to thirty days without joining a union—but on the thirty-first day, you've got to sign up or you're out of the show.

Method two is simply to buy your way into AFTRA, which since 1980 has been an "open union," meaning that you can join by showing up at union headquarters with your initiation fee and completing an application. AGVA, covering professional comics, singers, clowns, mimes, and other club artists, is also an open union that you can simply buy into (their initiation fee is currently $600) as long as you indicate "a desire to pursue a professional career." While AFTRA and AGVA memberships are easy to come by, getting one doesn't get you all that much, and for obvious reasons. Neither membership—by itself—will help you get into professional auditions, or into SAG or Equity by method three.

Method three is to "sister into" one union by being a working member of another. Under the "sister" provision, anyone who has been a member of SAG for a year or more can join Equity; Equity members, likewise after a year, can join SAG. But the "working member" criterion prevents you from simply converting your "bought" AFTRA card into a SAG or Equity card. Since AFTRA membership doesn't guarantee that you've actually worked as a professional actor, both SAG and Equity also require proof of actual employment—as a principal performer—under AFTRA's jurisdiction for those seeking to sister-in from AFTRA under this provision.

Method four is relatively new, and stems from SAG's recent absorption of the defunct Screen Extras Guild, or SEG. SAG now has exclusive jurisdiction over extras (also called "atmosphere players") in both film and television. Under the new provisions, film and television producers who employ extras must hire a certain minimum of them from SAG's membership: Currently the first fifteen extras hired each day for a TV show must be SAG members, as must the first thirty extras each day on a film. The remaining extras can be nonunion. So what's that got to do with your getting into the union? Occasionally, not enough union-hired extras actually show up on the set to make the production's legally-specified minimum, in which case the producer has to hire nonunion actors on a one-day union contract. So, get a nonunion extra gig, make a friend of the Assistant Director, and you might be the one picked to make the union minimum—in which case you'll get a SAG "voucher" indicating you've gotten hired for the day on a SAG contract. Pick up three of these vouchers, and you can join SAG. There's more about this under "Be an Extra" in Chapter 5.

Method five is Equity's *Membership Candidate Program*, which was created in 1978 as a logical stepping stone into the profession. And it is; no Equity program has been more successful in helping actors join the profession. This program provides that you can become eligible to join Equity by working as a nonunion actor or understudy for fifty weeks at any participating theatre operating under an Equity LORT, SPT, LOA, HAT, BAT, CAT, COST, CORST or U/RTA contract. At the COST and CORST theatres, understudying doesn't count—but being a production assistant to the Equity Stage Manager does. You can pass an Equity-administered test in lieu of the last ten weeks, too. You needn't be paid any set salary for this qualifying work, and you don't receive any Equity benefits: You're an Equity Membership Candidate, but not an Equity member during this time. If you can secure such employment—and remember to make certain the theatre company is participating in the program—you complete an application to join and submit a $100 registration fee (which will be credited to your eventual initiation fee) by certified check. When you complete your fifty weeks, you can join the union at any time in the next five years simply by paying the balance of the initiation fee (currently $800) and your first dues installment. Indeed, when you have completed forty weeks, you can take the test and, upon passing, join in the same manner. Note that non-resident aliens may not participate in this program.

Equity recommends that your Membership Candidate application be filed as soon as you start your work. Your application is an affidavit of non-professional status, and certifies that you "are interested in obtaining training for the theatre and/or intend to make a career in the professional theatre." You can then list "Equity Membership Candidate" in the space on your resume where union affiliation goes; this is not union affiliation, but at least it's something.

Your "open" AFTRA membership, obtained by method two, may, as noted before, actually *prevent* you from becoming an Equity Membership Candidate! Equity looks dimly on AFTRA members who have signed into AFTRA without actually working, and requires such AFTRA (or even former AFTRA) members to make a "special request" for permission to join the Membership Candidate program. "This request must contain a copy of your resume and a detailed description of your professional work history," Equity states. Only after such a review will Equity waive your "method two" AFTRA card, and permit you to come aboard through the Membership Candidate Program.

Method six, which is not really a method at all, but which is the way most people make it, is to keep battering at the doors every way you can. You can be seen, you can be auditioned, and you can be cast professionally without being in a union. It's harder, but it's obviously possible. It happens every day, and there's a lot of advice on how to do it in the pages that follow. There are doors that are closed, but there are always keyholes to peek through. Talent rises. And remember, if they find you and decide they want you, they'll hire you—they'll even pay a fine to hire you. Nobody's lack of union affiliation ever stopped a producer from trying to make a better movie, or a better play, or—let's face it—a bigger gross.

## Should You Join the Union?

Should you join a union? Yes—but . . .

It would be odd *not* to join the union if you had the chance, but there are some things to think about.

First, you must understand that being a member of the union means that you *cannot,* in most circumstances, accept nonunion work. Even finishing the Equity Membership Candidate program means this: Once you are in Equity, or have completed your fifty weeks as a Membership Candidate, you cannot, say, join the non-Equity acting company of a Shakespeare festival. So you're left home by the telephone while your friends are braving the Bard in Oregon or Lake Champlain. As a union member, your hands are a bit tied, unless you can finagle your way around (or beneath) your union's bylaws.

Probably, though, you will want to join at the first opportunity.

First of all, you're going to join anyway; you might as well do it when you get the chance. Second, you're going to want to support the efforts that will make your professional life easier: efforts to negotiate minimum wages and maximum working conditions, for example. And you're going to want to have easy access to the information sources that unions provide, including their own magazines, lobbies, bulletin boards, hot line telephone numbers, seminars, meetings, and informal networking services.

Where a union card will give you priority status in auditions, that's a plus too. Union (SAG) membership is still a virtual necessity in the film industry (although the NLRB is taking a hard look at SAG as well). And Equity membership still has a dominant cachet for stage producers, though they have equal legal obligations to nonunion actors. Habits are slow to change in this business.

But the main factors concerning union membership might be psychological. An Equity or SAG card makes you feel better about yourself and your career, and if you feel better you'll probably act better. Remember that "talent" is largely self-confidence, and card-carrying unionism, in this field, breeds professional pride. Rightly or wrongly, you'll walk a bit taller, and probably look a bit larger in other people's eyes as well. The fact is that most folks in show business simply assume, probably at the unconscious level, that only union membership conveys "big league" status, and that nonunion actors (EP or otherwise) are somewhere in the "minors." That's hardly the truth—or hardly the entire truth—but why fight it when you've got so many other battles yet to win?

## AGENTS AND AGENCIES

No character in the theatre or film industry arouses such contradictory attitudes as the agent. To the beginning actor, without contacts and without credits, the agent appears as a savior: the ultimate path to fame, fortune, and career. Actors fall all over themselves trying to get an agent to "represent" them, to "submit" them, to demonstrate their brilliance to the casting moguls, to do their hatchet work, spade work, telephoning, and interviewing.

But to the established actor, the agent is often the devil incarnate, the ubiquitous middleman with no interests—artistic or personal—but the inevitable 10% cut. A famous actor once paid his agency a commission of more than $10,000 in pennies, hauled up in an armored truck. Lawsuits and contract-breaking between actors and their agents are unfortunately common in this volatile industry. K. Callan begins both of her excellent books, *The N.Y. Agent Book* and *The L.A. Agent Book*, with discussions on why you should *leave* your agent. Dishonesty, lack of communication, failure to be sent out, and persistent thoughts of suicide head Callan's list. Also theft: "Stealing your money is a sound reason to leave. Stealing your trust is another."

Most agents are somewhere between saviors and thieves, however. For actors, the agent is at least an invaluable aid, and at most (particularly in Hollywood) a virtual necessity. So it's necessary to understand the agent—and agency—function.

An agent (the word comes from the Greek *agein,* "to drive") pushes forward (yes, "drives") your career, making his or her own income solely to the extent he or she helps you make yours.

The agent's job is to get you employment, and to negotiate the best possible salary for you. In return, the agent earns a percentage of what you do, ordinarily 10% of what you get through the agent's overtures. The agent *does not charge a fee* (if an agent proposes a fee, he or she isn't an agent!). If you don't work, the agent doesn't get paid, which creates some incentive for the agent to produce on your behalf. Even the 10% commission doesn't always kick in at lower income levels: In SAG–AFTRA work, the union will require you to be paid at least 10% more than "scale" so your agent's commission won't drag your fee down below minimum SAG standards. In Equity work at low-paying theatres (LORT B and below, off-Broadway, and so on), the agent's commission doesn't get paid until after ten weeks of performances; up to that time the agent gets a nominal flat rate ($50 to $100, depending on the theatre's size). This is one of the reasons why agents aren't as involved in stage work as they are in film: They don't get paid as much, or as often. Agent's fees aren't going to break your back, then, as a beginner, and you should certainly seek such a valuable business partner.

The role of agents and agencies and their importance varies significantly between New York and Hollywood, and between stage and camera actors. In New York, the agent is an important factor in most casting situations; in L.A. the agent is *crucial.* In Los Angeles, you simply *must* have an agent, preferably one with whom you have a signed, exclusive contract, in order to get serious work in films or television. In New York, the situation is quite a bit freer, and the relationships between agents and actors is considerably less formal. In New York you may be represented by several agents, but on an unsigned, free-lance basis.

What does an agent do for you? Basically, the agent "submits" you for private auditions—at film studios, with Broadway producers, and for television. These are not auditions that are posted anywhere, but rather auditions the agent knows about through private sources,

mainly through trade-circulated "breakdowns." No, this has nothing to
do with a mental collapse, though these are common in this business.
The Breakdown Service is a product available to agents only; it lists and
describes all the roles—by sex, age, and character type—in upcoming
TV episodic and movie-of-the-week scripts, and in a good number of
Broadway plays and feature film scripts as well. Obviously, to an actor,
these breakdowns—delivered every morning and cybermailed on the
Internet—are worth their weight in platinum, and they cost almost as
much. But you can't see them—not legally, anyway. Agents buy them,
and in buying them agree in writing not to show them to their actor
clients. Breakdowns help the agents focus their submittals and narrow
the range of actors they will submit for each role.

The agent also can arrange private interviews for you with casting
directors and other casting people. Obviously these will be several steps
above the cattle call situations that you (and everybody else) has read
about in the trades.

Why can't you arrange all these auditions and interviews yourself?
Why can't you just "submit yourself"? Because:

1. you don't have the breakdowns, so don't know the parts,
2. you don't have the contacts, so don't know the casting people,
   and
3. you don't have the credentials, since most casting people won't
   usually see you until an agent verifies that you're worth seeing.

So, you want—and probably need—an agent to represent and submit
you. Generally you want a formalized agency arrangement, usually with
an exclusive contract (always in L.A.; more often than not in New
York). You'll then redo your resumes, putting the agency logo and
phone number as your new point of contact; perhaps get some new
photos made while you're at it; and turn over a batch of these "new
and improved" photo-resumes to your agent, who will use them as calling cards for your submittals.

Your agent will then search through the breakdowns, and whatever
other casting information is available to the agency. (Lots of scripts
never turn up in the breakdowns, and lots of parts are written into TV
shows at the last minute; a good agent is always hustling for this kind of
information.) Then the agent will submit you to the appropriate producers or casting director for projects you might have a crack at getting into.

If a casting person bites, he or she will call the agent, the agent will
call you, and an interview and possibly an audition will be set up—not
necessarily at your convenience, of course. You will be given whatever
information the agent can get about the part (a SAG rule, rarely

enforced, says you must have 24 hours lead time to read the script—but the script may not be ready in time), and sometimes, if you are a particularly favored client, or the agent has the time and thinks it would be a good idea, your agent may personally escort you to the audition, introduce you to the producers, and try in other ways to grease the machinery for you. At that point, however, you are on your own. The interview and audition both depend on you. If you come through the audition and the inevitable callbacks with flying colors, somebody will call the agent back.

Here's another critical step. Your agent and a producer will negotiate your salary; surprisingly, perhaps, you may find you have little to say about it. If all goes well, your agent will get you the best salary the producer is willing to offer; the agent will then call you and tell you the terms. When you get paid, you give your agent whatever percentage of your gross income (the income paid to you before taxes are deducted) that your agency contract specifies.

So the actor-agent relationship is a good one when it works, and much of the time it *does* work. You are spending your time perfecting your craft, and your agent is hustling up and down Sunset Boulevard or Seventh Avenue looking for your future job.

But, of course, there are the inevitable wrinkles.

The agent can ignore you. An agent can take you on with marvelous promises, take a hundred photos and resumes, and never call you again. When this happens, you question why the agent took you on in the first place. What may have happened is that you have a highly unusual look and the agent simply wanted to file your pictures away until a call came in for just that look—and the call never arrived. Or the next day the agent may have found someone just like you but "better." Or the agent may have had other designs on your company which you, unwittingly, did not oblige (it's a real world out there, folks). There can be *any number* of reasons why an agent takes you on and then ignores you, and it happens all the time. That's why Ms. Callan begins her book on how to get an agent with advice on how to leave one. If you haven't signed a contract, you've lost nothing but your photos; just start looking for somebody else. If you've signed a contract, you've got to start pushing your agent to get on the stick. Standard agency contracts allow you to terminate your representation if you have not received 10 days of work in your first 151 days, or in any subsequent 91-day period, but if the agent isn't working out, you can probably negotiate an amicable withdrawal sooner than that.

The agent can promote you for the wrong roles. Agents are not simply clearing offices; they are second-guessers. They do their own breakdowns, of course; you've got to make sure they don't break *you* down. "I admit, we play God," confesses one. Well, they *have* to. An agent can't send fifty clients for a single reading—he or she would never get a call again. Remember, most agents know what they're doing; most are *objective* about your chances, and most probably know how to market you best. But sometimes they don't.

(You may be offended at the terms agents use: You are part of their "stable" of talent, you are "marketed" like a cabbage, you are a "juvenile female" instead of an actress—you will have to learn to live with this, too.)

The agent can be too greedy on your behalf. An actor who sings and plays the guitar was offered a terrific contract at a prestigious New York nightclub, where many celebrities got their starts. He had, however, recently signed with an agent who persuaded him he should get more money. He demanded what she said, the offer was withdrawn, and he never had the chance again. (Shed no tears; he went on to direct *Who's the Boss?*) Other agents go well beyond persuading you to overreach your salary potential; they demand it in your name without even consulting you. Since the agent bargains directly with the producer before you do, your agent can keep you out of roles you have successfully auditioned for. No matter that you would work for free in order to get that first credit. Your agent may negotiate you right out of it by demanding an extra $100. You may see this as just the chance you take—after all, the agent is interested in the same thing you are, right? Not exactly. The agent is interested in your *income*, which is not always the same as your total artistic and career growth. The best agents are interested in that, too; the greedy ones want their cut and they want it now. Sympathize with them; they have big phone bills. But be alert. Your best interests and theirs are not always exactly the same. You have the final option, if you demand it. Gary Shaffer, casting director for various movies-of-the-week, advises, "If you want to be an actor, have your agent submit you for everything. Don't worry about pay. Tell him not to turn down *anything*."

Finally, an agent can simply give you bad advice. In that, the agent is no more guilty than anybody else you may come across, but it hurts more when your agent advises you badly because you feel obligated to take the advice. In fact, you probably *are* obligated to take it if you want the agent to help you. But the agent is not always the most objective observer of the industry. Remember that agents are often former (or failed) actors, and sometimes they have their own axes to grind—and they may just grind them on you. They may also be in a bad mood; understand that despite their savior status in some aspirants' minds, agents do not live a very heavenly life. They spend most of their time nagging casting people, bugging receptionists for scraps of information, and being put on HOLD; sometimes they will take their frustration out on their clients, which means on you. So, in their offices, *they* know all the answers: how you should act, what your pictures should look like, what acting teacher you should study with, how right you are for what role, and how much weight you should lose. Now, in all honesty, your agent is *probably* right. But the *degree* of probability is not as great as most agents would have you believe.

Knowing the wrinkles, should you try to get an agent? Of course, you should. The agent is on the inside of the business and you aren't. Some are more careful, likable, honest, and well known than others, but all franchised agents have access to important contacts and information that you don't. In New York, most important casting is done through agencies; in Hollywood virtually *all* casting is. In Hollywood, indeed, the agent has virtually become a producer, so involved have the agencies grown in packaging and planning film and television productions. Forget the cigar chomping, ex-vaudevillian image; Hollywood agents now tend to be college graduates and business people; they are the power brokers of the film world.

## Finding and Getting an Agent

There are literally hundreds of agents and agencies in both L.A. and New York (there are some in other cities as well, though not of similar importance), and agencies vary enormously in their practical worth—particularly for an actor who's starting out. The difference between having a career and not having one can quite easily depend on which door you knock on first.

Many agents work in their own offices and handle an absolute minimum of clients. One, for example, handles only six. You needn't worry about him, though; four of those six make more than $3 million a year. The other two are expected "comers." Obviously, that is the kind of agent you want. Also, obviously, that is not the kind of agent you're going to get. Not yet, anyway.

Other agents work in the huge prestige "star" agencies, of which there are currently two: Creative Artists Agency (CAA) and International Creative Management (ICM), with the historic William Morris Agency (WMA, but generally simply known by its name) now climbing back up to a top-ranking position after some bad years. Each of these has offices in New York and L.A. just for starters, and include upwards of fifty to a hundred agents in each office. The smaller UTA (United

Talent Agency) and Endeavor have recently emerged to form some-thing of a second list. While there's a lot of movement to and fro between actors and agents (and agents and agencies), the last time I checked, CAA clients included film stars Kevin Costner, Tom Cruise, Jack Nicholson, Nathan Lane, Sylvester Stallone, Madonna, and Barbra Streisand. ICM, headed by Jeffrey Berg, has enjoyed the strongest list of actresses in recent years, including at various times Julia Roberts, Andie McDowell, Anjelica Huston, Rebecca De Mornay, Jennifer Jason Leigh, Susan Sarandon, Helen Mirren, and Marlee Matlin. The William Morris Agency has recently represented, among a few thou-sand others, familiar names like Whitney Houston, John Travolta, Clint Eastwood, Bill Cosby, and Emma Thompson. UTA counts Jim Carrey and Sandra Bullock as clients. And Harrison Ford is the sole client of Patricia McQueeney, who has represented him since 1970. It may do your ego good to be contracted by these agencies, but you can get lost in there: Top agents must handle a few million dollars of business each year to pay their overhead and make their living, and 10% of Kevin Costner's earnings are going to go a lot further to those ends than 10% of yours, so Costner's agent isn't exactly the sort of person who will be spending a lot of time with you, even if you were somehow to become a client. Which would be unlikely in any case: Star agencies are those you work your way into, not get discovered by.

For a beginning actor, it is almost certainly best to ignore the big-ger agencies (which will ignore you in any event) and to hunt out the small, aggressive, hungrier operations that look at untried talent and have the time and inclination to develop a genuine interest in your development. Only then will the actor–agent relationship—a marriage in many ways—prove truly fruitful.

How do you pick an agent to call? First of all, the agent must be franchised. In Hollywood this means franchised at least by the Screen Actors Guild, and in New York by the Actors' Equity Association—but preferably your agency should be franchised by all three unions. Any of the three union offices will give you lists of their franchised agents (sometimes for a nominal charge), and under no circumstances should you sign with a nonfranchised one; franchised agencies will have a license on the wall. Beware: Phony "talent agencies" spring up every year, charging fees (no legitimate agent charges any fee), or requiring you to use the company photographer (usually somebody's brother-in-law) and/or to attend a "class" or "workshop" prior to sign-ing on. These are positively *illegal:* Franchised agencies may not require that you use specified photographers, nor may they operate schools. Alert the appropriate union if you are approached for this scam. The state labor commissioner will do something about it.

So, you have a list of franchised agents. Still, a list is only a list, and it will be an unwieldy one: There are more than 200 actor agencies in Los Angeles alone. Some of them you will probably want to stay clear of. Though franchised and legal, these specialize in celebrities of somewhat less than Emmy–Oscar–Tony calibre. One such enterprise represents a stable of talent that includes such questionable thesps as Kato Kaelin, John Wayne Bobbitt, Tonya Harding, Gennifer Flowers, and Tammy Faye Bakker. When signing a man primarily famous for admitting to a particularly egregious statutory rape and a consequent solicitation of murder, the agency put out a press release proudly announcing that "this agency, which . . . always will stand for quality and talent, has signed Joey Buttafuoco in all fields. . . . With the loss of John Belushi and John Candy, there is a need for a really dedicated actor who can play drama and comedy with ease." You might think twice about joining up with this one. But how do you find the ones that are right for you?

First, and obviously, if you have some friends in the industry, ask them for suggestions. Can someone recommend an agent or an agency to you? That's good. And if so, can that friend also recommend you to the agency? That's positively great! I'll come back to that in a moment.

You can check out the books listed in the appendix (or more current ones you can find in the drama bookshops) that list and describe —and sometimes rank or rate—the agencies. *The Working Actors Guide*, for example, lists agencies and describes what they might be looking for. ("Adults only. Prefers mailed submissions; no drop-offs and no follow-up calls," says one; "Looking for newcomers age 18 through 20. Looks at submissions only through referral," says another; "Accepts infants from 14 days old through young adults. Mailed submissions— headshot or 3/4 bodyshots—only, no drop-offs and no follow-up calls. Will view VHS tapes only by recommendation. Handles nonunion newcomers for commercials," says a third.)

Thumb through the pages (or click your way through the CD-ROM) of the actor photolistings in *Players Directory*, which you can access in Hollywood (see the appendix) or the similar *Players Guide* in New York, which will show you the working actors there and tell which agencies represent them. Check out the agencies that seem to employ actors like you. You will get, from this exercise, some sort of picture of which agents are handling which kinds of clients, and you will certainly get a sharper idea of where to start.

From these sources you should be able to compile a couple of lists: a short list of ten to twenty smallish agencies that might handle people like yourself, and a long list of perhaps a hundred that just *might* take you on. You can begin, if you like, by making a mass mailing—a photo/resume and cover letter—to all of those on your long list. But I'd suggest working on your short list to start. Write or call on them—in ways that they themselves might suggest in literature you can find. And see if you can connect through a personal contact. There is that dirty word again—sorry, but it's more important here than ever. The biggest agents won't see *anybody* without some personal reference, and a personal reference from somebody important at that. Your best chance of getting an agent, if you can swing it, is to be recommended by a working producer. And get the *producer* to set up the appointment if you can (if you can't, at least get permission to use the producer's name, and an understanding that the agent can call the producer to verify). If a producer is behind you, the agent will feel that you already have a leg up on getting work; besides, by taking you on, the agent may be able to broaden his or her *own* contacts at the same time. Remember, like you, the agent is always looking for ways to strengthen contacts. But even if the contact is just another actor who recommends that you see his or her agent (which, ordinarily, only an actor of the opposite sex is likely to do), the personal contact is an invaluable way to get your foot in the door.

When the short list is exhausted, you can make a mass mailing to all the agents in either town, using preaddressed mailing labels available for a modest charge in the drama bookshops in both New York and L.A. (see the appendix). With a smashing photo, and/or outstanding professional credits, you can often get an interview on the spot. Arthur Rosenberg, a fine character actor, came to Hollywood with five years of solid LORT credits on his resume. He sent photo-resumes to the more than 200 agents then in Hollywood, and received seventeen invitations to interview. This led to two offers to sign. You only have to do half as well as Rosenberg, since it only takes *one* offer to get an agent—but his extensive professional credits were crucial.

If you lack a personal contact or extensive professional credits, your next best means of landing an agent is to be *seen* in something. This involves getting a fairly good role in a showcase. The name says it all: You may be paid little or nothing (you may even have to pay), but you are "shown" in a "case"—you are put on display for all comers. Showcases come in many forms. The best are probably regular plays, particularly at nearby regional theatres, off-off-Broadway in New York, the Equity–Waiver (technically "99-seat Theatre Plan") productions in

L.A. (so-called because only 99 seats are allowed, and actors—even union actors—are paid as little as $5 a performance, waiving the normal Equity scale minimums), and even community theatre and amateur productions, if they're good enough.

Membership companies provide particularly popular showcasing opportunities in Los Angeles; these are theatre groups you can join (membership is competitive, of course), pay dues to, and then showcase yourself in the company's season of regular performances. Theatre 40, the Colony Theatre, and Group Repertory Theatre are among the better known such companies.

Then there are named "showcases" that aren't plays at all, but simply collections of scenes and monologues put together for an evening strictly to show off the participating actors to an invited audience of casting people; normally there's a catered reception—or wine and cheese—following to permit some socializing between would-be actors and the agents and casting directors. Some drama schools and departments present such actor showcases in L.A. and New York—sometimes in various consortia of several schools—for their graduates. Other, strictly commercial showcases (also known as "industry nights" or "agents' nights") have been created for actors who pay to get into them, in L.A. particularly. You pay a fee (usually $100 to $500) in return for promised attendance by casting people, who may be paid an "honorarium" to show up. Commercial showcases have a mixed reputation, however. Rob Kendt, editor of *Back Stage West,* found that most L.A. actors have been dissatisfied with their commercial showcase experience, with some complaining that they "smell of influence peddling" or even kickbacks. Not all are well-performed or well-attended, and some agents and casting directors have stopped attending them. "I've seen so many showcases that just sucked so much that I didn't care to remember anybody who was in them, because they were such horrible experiences," one agent says. "If a showcase isn't done right, leftover food is about all an actor gets out of it," says Kendt. The quality of the whole showcase—and not just your scene in it—is crucial to everyone's success. Adds James Calleri, casting director for Playwrights' Horizons in New York, "Remember, you're only as good as the worst person in the showcase." But casting does sometimes occur by this route, and it's certainly worth considering. You and a few friends can even create your own showcase, by hiring a theatre, producing the show, catering a reception, and then marketing the evening for all it's worth. It doesn't matter who produces the showcase, but it does matter who comes. The test of a showcase is the number of agents and casting people who actually arrive and see the show. Ticket prices should be low, comp tickets generously given (they are *required* to be given to cast-ing professionals), and the industry audience should be assiduously courted.

Getting a good part in a showcase is not by any means automatic, but you can quickly find your way around to their auditions. In New York, the trade papers and the *Village Voice* are excellent sources of information; in Los Angeles, *Drama-Logue* and *Back Stage West* will let you know what is going on. When you get your showcase role, you should do everything you can to attract attention (that's the whole point of doing it)—so print up and mail out flyers and invitations (you can print your photos on these if you want), solicit RSVPs, send photo-postcard reminders, arrange limousine transportation for reluctant agents (some showcases provide valet parking and buffet meals!), and even pay for advertisements in the trade papers. Follow-up is crucial. If you get good trade reviews, you can print up new photo-postcard invi-tations, highlighting your reviews, and send out a second round. Show-cases should always record the industry people who attend (ordinarily a sign-in book is provided in the lobby); all of these should get a follow-up letter from you—and, if all else fails, a phone call. If you're good and have professional potential, they'll get back to you.

Agents and casting people do see showcases, some as often as three or four a week. Showcases are your best first way of getting seen at *work*, and paid work really does come out of them if you touch all the right bases.

## Interviewing an Agent

Once you have an agent interested in you, you'll probably be asked in for an interview. The interview is crucial; it will determine if the agent takes you on. Since you will also be interviewing for roles later on, you must treat the interview with the agent just as seriously as an interview with a producer or director. The agent will be trying to see if you inter-view as well as you act, and it is important that you do.

If you are invited to "come in and talk," set up an appointment and keep it exactly. Arrive on time, and look your best. Be yourself, but be clean, neat, and striking. "Look like an actor and act like an actor," sug-gests one agent. Be at ease and be positive. Agents aren't necessarily any good at interviewing; they may be awkward and nervous just like you. *Help* the agent interview you. Don't just wait for questions: Describe your career, your desires, your commitment, your training, what you feel you can do, and what sacrifices you are prepared to make. Don't ham it up, but be active, infectious; obviously an agent will be more interested in you if it appears that you have what it takes to generate a career.

Impress the agent that you want to become a working professional actor, and that you have a realistic outlook about the business, and about your future. Don't presume to know more about show business than the agent does, and don't fret openly about your recent failures, whatever they may be. Offer to audition; most agents will see an audition in their office, and you should have a monologue prepared. Offer to come back in with a scene—but have a rehearsed scene and scene partner ready for just such occasions.

Ask some questions, too. How does the agent see you? How does the agent see using you? Each agent has a particular point of view, and an agent whose plan to use you doesn't ring the bells may prove worse than no agent at all. You want an agent who, regardless of his or her standing, is enthusiastic about you, and sees you pretty much the way you want to be seen. If you want to play classical tragedy and the agent wants to sell you for soap opera, you had better get things straight before you sign. No agent will be offended if you simply ask: "How do you see me?" Let him or her tell you; you may be astonished at what you hear. Give your agent the benefit of the doubt, if there is one. You might, amazingly, prove to be a lot better in *As the World Turns* than in *As You Like It.* On the other hand, you may not want to spend the rest of your life in the soaps, so you have some decisions to make.

Close the interview when you think you have said and asked everything on your mind. Know when to quit talking, and offer to leave (it's best to be leaving "for an audition at Universal" than "for an appointment at the dentist's").

The agent will probably *not* offer you a contract on the spot. He or she may want to think you over, to consult with colleagues, to see you do additional work, and/or to check the files for available jobs in your line. If the agent doesn't grab you on the way out, he or she might well call you later. Your task is simply to hang in there until something happens.

And then it does happen: An agent decides to take you on as a client. In L.A. you will normally sign an exclusive contract for the agent to represent you in all *dramatic* camera media. Later you may get another agent for commercials, and yet another for live theatre, although some agents will handle all three. In New York you *may* be asked to sign an exclusive contract, or the agent may simply take you on as a free-lance client, in which case you can work with several agents.

Should you sign up or free-lance? It's probably best to sign—that way, the agent is more committed to you, and you to the agent. Also the agent will probably think of you before going to his or her free-lance list. An agent who sends a free-lancer up for a role first has to confirm the submission with the actor, to make sure that the actor hasn't already been submitted by another agent; this takes time, and the agent may not want to bother with the extra phone call. But signing up is also signing away; it's a major career decision, something like a marriage, and you should feel pretty good about it before going ahead. Your initial agency contract will normally be for one year; subsequent resignings are typically for three years.

When you sign with an agent, you have entered into a partnership you both hope will prove beneficial to both of you. But *you have by no means "made it"*; you are still just beginning.

A good agent will take a serious interest in your career. He or she will get your pictures into the *Players Directory* or *Players Guide* (though you will probably pay the fee), and will seek out casting opportunities, through breakdown services and other sources available only to agencies. The agent will, to some extent, be the manager of your career—even if you have a manager (see below). It is vital, therefore, that you establish a trusting relationship. This may take some patience on your part. One agent cautions, "It may take a year or so to establish you in the overall market picture, and another two years to get offers coming in with any regularity. The third year is usually when the payoff comes—if it does." If you are hoping for instant results, you may be very frustrated. Actors who impatiently switch agents every six months only have to begin over and over again, and never establish an image in the industry.

If you are lucky enough to find an agent who sees you the way you wish to be seen, an agent in whom you feel confident, sign up and follow the agent's advice. Accept his or her judgment on your photographs, what you should wear, how you should do your hair, how much weight you should lose, and so forth. Talk things over, but be prepared to trust. Nobody's advice is perfect, but your agent is your partner, and the two of you should be working together, or not at all.

And don't settle back! Just because you have an agent, you can't afford to become a passive participant in your own career. You are still going to have to make your rounds, get yourself known, get involved, and generate your network of contacts. You're also going to have to energize your own agent! As William Bayer explains, "Hustle your hustler. You're going to have to sell and pressure and hustle just as much with an agent as without one; you're going to have to continue to excite your agent, because the moment he gets bored, there's nothing in it for either of you." Exasperating? Yes, but true. Your agent needs reinforcement when putting your name out there. He or she needs casting people to *glow* at the mention of your name, not stare blankly in quizzical puzzlement. And that means getting known—making your rounds.

## MANAGERS

Should you have a manager? Some actors now turn to personal managers and business managers to advise them in their careers. Managers do not replace agents (a manager cannot negotiate a contract, only a franchised agent can), so your fee to the manager, which is usually 15% of your income and can include a flat fee besides, is *in addition* to your agent's commission. And most of what a manager will do should be done by your agent anyway. Ordinarily, then, you should *not* get involved with a manager. But there are some exceptions. Some people who should have a manager include (1) very successful actors, who need business guidance, (2) actors in whose future a potential manager has made a substantial cash proposition, and (3) actors for whom the manager offers valuable services available no other way. There are, certainly, occasions when a manager will be so skilled, so enthusiastic and committed on your behalf, and so successful in making and using professional contacts to benefit your career, that his or her help will prove vital. Finding when this situation exists, however, is the trick— and it's a puzzler. What professional contacts does a manager really have? Show business, remember, is name-dropper land. You might need to hire a professional investigator to find this one out. Best to avoid a manager, unless very compelling evidence suggests the reverse.

## ROUNDS: SEEING THE CDS

What do actors do when they are not working? They go on rounds. This is as time-honored as the opening-night party at Sardi's. It means going to see everybody and anybody who can get them a job in the theatre. These days, it basically means going to see casting directors.

The casting director is a relatively new creature in the theatrical world, brought into existence, among other reasons, by the fact that there are just so many of you (actors) out there that directors and producers don't have the time to find out about you—they're too busy directing and producing.

Casting directors (CDs) are employed by studios, by individual film and television production companies, by Broadway and off-Broadway producers, and by most regional theatres. Sometimes they are part of a permanent staff (as at the Universal Studios casting department); more often they are free-lancers, with their own New York and L.A. offices, hired for individual projects. Their job is to recommend, out of the hundred thousand–plus professional actors, the two or three that the director and producer will want to see. You want to be in that two or three, naturally.

It is the CD's goal to find the best talent for the project or company he or she is working for. It's your goal to convince the CD that that's you, but the CD has to see you first.

Casting directors *want* to know the work of every actor in the business; it's their *job* to know you if you're any good, and it's also their job to know how to get in touch with you. They go to showcases all the time, therefore, as well as to screenings and theatre productions (Broadway, off-Broadway, LORT, depending on where they're located), and they also watch television—they probably watch more television than anybody in the business.

They also see actors in their own casting offices when they have time, and your rounds are basically rounds of those offices. Most CDs give general office auditions, and the first step in your rounds is to write all the casting directors in town—in New York or L.A., that is—and ask for an appointment. Your letter should be brief but interesting, and your photo-resume should be a grabber. Your agent, if you have one, will help you with all this, but you can often see a CD without an agent; you can write to a CD directly for an interview, just as you write to an agent.

Locating CDs is not difficult; seeing them, of course, is another matter. Theatre bookshops in both L.A. and New York will have several books listing—and in some cases describing—the CDs in town and what they cast: Those put out by Breakdown Services and Acting World Books (L.A.) and the Ross Reports (N.Y.) are the most reliable and most frequently updated (see the appendix for further information). The Acting World listings, as well as *The Working Actors Guide* in L.A., will also provide updated information on which CDs are willing to take submissions, and from whom. Certain issues of *Back Stage* and *Back Stage West* also have such listings and descriptions.

Your CD interview is likely to be similar to an agent's interview, and you should be prepared to present an audition. It's a good idea to have several pieces ready (see "Auditions" in the next chapter), but you should know which one you want to do as your signature audition first —and the others only if asked.

You should also have some extra photos to leave off, and this is a great time to bring your demo reel if you have one. Be prepared to leave it, and be sure you have your name, address, and phone number written on it. (Indeed, some actors carry around a stamped, self-addressed cassette-carrying envelope for its return.)

Do you go on CD rounds even though you have an agent? Absolutely—the agent can help you only so far. The ultimate initiative must be yours, and you have to keep at it. "If you stop pushing for one minute, they forget you," says actress Terri Garr. "You're out. Gone, goodbye!" Don't wait to be asked; go for the interview. Audition! A casting director has described for me one particularly successful actor in these words:

> He works a lot because he *never* stops plugging. He makes job hunting a full-time occupation. He has an excellent agent, but he gets himself one-half of his jobs! Everyday he goes to one studio, dropping by to just say "Hi!" to the casting people, so he will be fresh in their minds. He reads the trades every day to see what new projects are beginning and who is involved. He then immediately goes to see them, no matter how big they are (both Robert Wise and Mike Nichols have thrown him out of their offices!). He's got a lot of *chutzpah*—a true necessity. He marches right through (or drives right through) the studio gates: You can go *anywhere* if you look like you belong, so simply wave at the studio guard.

So rounds become your day-to-day lifestyle in New York or Hollywood.

Since you are literally going to be seeing *dozens* of agents and CDs in your first year in the business, you should *log* your rounds. Some actors do this in a notebook, others in a card file. Your log should list the date you submitted each photo-resume, and where; the date you visited each agent and casting office; the names of the people you spoke with, and their suggestions for following up, if any. You will want to pay repeat visits to some agencies, but you will have to space these out so as not to become a pest. Don't count on your memory for very much, because you can visit and forget several offices a day, and come home with only the foggiest idea of where you've been or what you've accomplished.

## CD Workshops, Classes, and Seminars

It has recently become the fashion for CDs to offer, at a price, work-shops and seminars in auditioning, and showcases to which other CDs are invited. These activities are in sort of a gray area morally, for while the CD clearly is able to offer you sound advice on how to audition, you are also, quite obviously, paying to be seen, and paying the person you hope will hire you. This comes awfully close to bribery—yet it is gener-ally conducted in an above-board manner, and work does come out of it. You should investigate these seminars carefully, and make certain you are actually getting your money's worth *in instruction* before sign-ing on. You should also check the CD's credentials; after all, anyone can *claim* to be a CD, and yet be just as much an unemployed beginner as you are. (CDs, unlike agents, are not franchised.) The fees for such workshops should also be in line with other such professional classes advertised in the trades; if they're substantially above that, take a *very* close look.

## GETTING KNOWN: ADVERTISEMENTS FOR YOURSELF

With or without an agent, and with or without a union card, you must get known and get seen. You must market yourself. Making rounds is a form of self-marketing and self-advertisement. So is getting your pic-ture into the *Players Directory*, if you work out of Los Angeles, although you must have an acting union card and be represented by a SAG-franchised agent to do this. "We open that book a hundred times a day," says Jerold Franks, casting director for Columbia Pictures. If you meet the qualifications, you can have your headshot, plus a listing of some of your special skills (see the appendix), published in the *Direc-tory* for a nominal price: $25 per issue in 1997 (there are three issues a year, both in book form and CD-ROM). The comparable *Player's Guide* in New York, which went out of business in 1996, is returning to the field as this book goes to press and promises to be circulating client photos by book, CD-ROM, and Website by the time you read this.

You can also get your photo and resume on the net if you want; a variety of services will put you there, such as Actors Online (at http://www.actorsOnline.com). You can, for that matter, create your own website with your photo and resume, and even snippets of your demo reel if you have one; there are services that will help you do that, too. But beware: Internet services for actors are in their infancy at the time of writing (early 1997), and neither they nor an individual Web-site will, by themselves, garner you very much real attention. What these sites actually deliver is your photo and resume—to someone who already wants them. But this person has to know about you first, and few if any casting directors are currently cruising the Net looking for unknowns—at least not for acting roles. At the moment, even the biggest actor–Internet services have only a tiny fraction (far less than 1%) of the country's professional actors on display, and they're competing fiercely with each other for the right to sign up any and all new-comers. Still, the Internet is surely the wave of the future in this field, given its instant and world-wide access and its capability for up-to-the-minute updates.

Photo-postcards make effective quickie advertisements that can circulate your picture under the guise of an otherwise ordinary com-munication. Your photo and name, printed on one side, accompanies your message (and the address of the person to whom you're writing) on the other. Such postcards, which you can have made in bulk, are a good way to confirm dates, thank people for their attention and con-sideration, and announce your current activities to those who've expressed some interest in hearing about them. Postcards also have the advantage of being easily thumbtacked to a wall if anybody wants to look at you for a day or two—and who knows but that they might?

Then there's the bolder approach. Advertise in print. The most discreet advertising is done by stars, who pay high fees to take space in *Variety* to "congratulate" the magazine on its anniversary (and make clear the star is still alive, kicking, and available). Stars also become the spokespersons for charities that will keep their name before the public, and raise the moral standard of their reputations.

You probably can't become a charity spokesperson yet, but an ad promoting your successful appearance in a showcase is very worth-while. Elaine Partnow, a Los Angeles actress, capitalized on her perfor-mance in a workshop production by using some of her reviews, which were in the "brilliant" category, to put together a quarter-page ad in (Daily) *Variety*. Then she made up 800 reproductions of the ad and sent them to every producer and director in television, and every Equity theatre in the country. The result: two phone calls. At $200 a call, that's an expensive way to get known, but two phone calls are, after all, better than none. And you're not limited to postcards and quarter-pages, either. One Alma Kessler paid $10,000 to put her face (six times life-size) on billboards over Sunset Boulevard, with the leading line "Who is Alma Kessler and what's her game?" "Why did you do it?" she was asked. "I love show business," she replied. "I've always wanted to be a performer. I'm 50, and I'm free, so it's now or never. I've got to be a star. So it costs money? So what's money?" We may still be asking, "Who is Alma Kessler?," but it's not for want of effort. Taking out an advertisement for yourself can be an expensive and sometimes humiliating experience. But you must get known—and at a certain point, as Ms. Kessler pointed out, it's "now or never."

## Chapter 5

# On the Move: Interviews, Auditions, and Getting the Job

## INTERVIEWS

Interviews are as much a make-or-break step on the road to getting a role as any other single act. An interview may take place through your initiative, or when a CD or producer has called *you*. In this latter (happy) case, you at least know you are in competition for a role that actually exists, even if you may be but one out of many who are called.

How important are interviews versus auditions? In Hollywood, interviews are often more important, because CDs and directors are mostly looking for what they call your "quality," which is to say your looks, personality, and personal charisma, and probably including your sex appeal. Thus, most of the competition is weeded out at the interview stage—prior to any actual auditioning. Indeed, in television and film (and sometimes even in theatre) there is often *no* audition; casting commitments are made at the interview stage (or even in the agent-producer negotiations) alone. Many veteran film actors even make it a point of personal privilege never to audition; they just meet the producer and/or director, who either is already familiar with their work or who can call up a film or two from studio vaults.

Interviews are a great stumbling block for many actors. "I don't interview well," is a common complaint, and actors capable of playing characters with strength, compassion, and subtlety fall to pieces when they are asked to play themselves.

For that's what you do in an interview: You play yourself. You must not think for a moment that an interview is simply a casual, obligatory preface to an audition. The interview is a stage on which million-dollar decisions are made, and despite the general (and desirable) state of apparent informality in which they usually take place, you are being examined very closely—and you must truly perform.

The interview is calculated to let the casting people know just what kind of person you are. Film and television directors may rely particularly on your personal quality rather than your acting: "Casting people are *afraid* of people who act," is an occasionally voiced Hollywood complaint. Because of the extremely limited rehearsal time for most television shows (and many films and plays, for that matter), producers are always partial to the actor whose own personality closely matches the characterization they want. You must remember that they have literally *thousands* of people to choose from; so why should they take someone who's 6'3" when they are looking for someone who's 6'2"? Casting decisions are rarely that specific as to height, of course, but if you translate that into subjective qualities, you begin to see how little compromise they have to make.

How should you "perform" in an interview? Boldly. You play yourself, to be sure, but you are entitled to select *which* aspects of yourself you want to display. Be yourself, but be your *best* self. You are an actor: Look like it and act like it. You are a *professional:* Let them know that too. Arrive well ahead of time, prepared with extra copies of your photo-resume (even though you've sent one ahead), a cassette demo tape if you can, and a book of pictures of yourself. Relax and let your salable qualities shine.

Don't just sit back and wait for something to happen, however— *make it happen.* "If you were on the other side of the desk," says casting director Mike Hanks, "and you were looking for talent, what would really interest you? It's that little spark. It's really in the eye of the beholder, some little spark you see in somebody that makes them exciting, interesting, that you can identify with." So ask questions. Be vivacious, not retiring. Be friendly but not self-effacing. Be funny, if you feel like it, but not at your own (or their) expense. In short, sell yourself without blasting them out of the room.

Be polite, but don't *rely* on being polite. Don't simply wait for questions and then meekly answer them; this is not a criminal investigation. Initiate questions and start the conversation yourself, when it seems possible and appropriate. You are not a butterfly mounted on a pin, a patient etherized upon a table; you have to *live* during the interview.

What will you face? You can never predict for sure: usually a casting director, perhaps a producer (maybe two or three), and maybe a secretary or another actor who happens to be in the room with you. You may be introduced to everyone; try to remember their names (and when you leave the office, write them down for future reference). Your first look when you walk in the door tells them 75% of what they wanted to know already, so make that first look a good one. Be confident, be attractive, and show those things you consider to be your personal assets. Then sit down and get them to talk to you.

Without fail you will hear, "Well, tell me about yourself." There it is: the one big identity question that has shrivelled some actors into their own neuroses so far that they can only stammer their name, rank, and Social Security number. Be prepared for it. There are no rules for interviews, no forms to fill out. If you begin by telling them all your problems, the interview is over before it begins. "Well, I suppose you want to know about my credits. I don't have any." Only a psychologist can explain why so many actors destroy themselves by such remarks. Tell them about yourself—honestly, but positively, infectiously: "I want to become a working professional actor . . . I played Coriolanus at Ashland . . . I write features for *Surfer* magazine." Of course you're insecure, but don't let it show. Don't ask, "Would it be all right if I . . . ?" It's not all right if you have to ask, so just go ahead and do it, whatever it is. Tell them things you would like them to know, and avoid things you would rather they did not know. Nobody has asked you to present both sides of the case, after all; they have every reason in the world *not* to cast you, so don't make that decision any easier for them. *Never* be desperate.

Positive personality, not repetition of facts, provides the content of the good interview. Richard Dreyfuss says of his successful first interviews, "I would try to take over . . . in the sense of going beyond those questions . . . I would *ask* questions. I would ask questions about the script, I would give them my opinion about the script. I would let them see as much of Rick Dreyfuss as possible, rather than just the information of my history."

You have to be memorable, above all. CDs and producers see a great many people when casting, so you have to stand out in their memory—some way or other. If you can look memorable, or say something memorable, or do something memorable, it helps. Mere politeness (which, after all, you must practice) is not enough to stimulate anybody's interest; *everybody* is polite. A downright hostile attitude, though not recommended, is better than stolid numbness. Be attractively unique, a bit dangerous. Find an exciting way to be different.

Show them that beneath your nice exterior, and your professional calm, lies the fire of passion and charisma.

And while casting-couch sex is almost always out of bounds these days, carefully sharing your sexually-correct sex appeal is certainly not. While producer Lynda Obst may feel that nobody sleeps his or her way to the top anymore (see the previous chapter), she also considers flirting an "essential tool." Obst is speaking of "tactical flirting . . . walking the line between virtual and actual seduction." The casting couch, it seems, has now become the casting gaze. As Obst explains, "With eyes focused on her prey, she makes the other the most interesting person in the world, as though the person were a real date. His interests interest her. His past movies are among her favorites. The point is to make him see that she is fun to work with because she *likes* him and that she's not looking to find fault or to judge him." Whether this is flirting or just agreeability may be a matter of semantics. Of one thing Obst is sure: "No clothing is ever removed . . . because nobody really [goes all the way]."

Interviewing takes practice. You should go to every interview you can, because with each you will acquire not only valuable know-how, but an unfakable confidence. It may take ten or fifteen interviews before you will really start to "come out," since the tendency of most sensitive people (and most actors *are* sensitive people) is to sit docilely and be inoffensive, just plain nice. Some of that is just nerves, face it. If you leave your interview breathing a deep sigh of relief, you've probably blown it. Conversely, if you leave feeling excited, feeling that you've met some interesting people, well then, they probably feel the same way about you, and you've probably done very well.

Here's an informative stream-of-consciousness report on the subject, from a young actor currently making headway in his career:

> Initial office report, the complexity of the office—well it's difficult to get on to it but you MUST get right on to it, right away. It's a fine line, a very fine line. You have to be up, funny, likable, charming, and impressive, and yet a little bit vulnerable, and hopefully a tiny bit naive, but you can't think about *any* of that, you just have to be your own natural self, and you're being eyeballed every second—they just want to hear you talk, and that's why so many lead-off questions are "Hi, Bruce, tell me about yourself!" What could be worse? You don't know where to start. "Well, I'm a new actor, new in town, and I hope for the best. . . ." No one wants to hear that, but what they want to hear is a relaxed, calm, involved person, an "on" person. But you can't be too on, too

up—well, this all has to be learned. Some love it, some hate it. I love it because I'm into people and I love people and that's where you meet them—all sorts of new people—in the office.

Here's another, from a similarly successful young actor two years into a professional career:

> Perhaps the most important thing I have learned in working professionally is that "to succeed" the prime ingredient is confidence. This is not overconfidence or bravura or telling everyone what a success you're going to be. The confidence I'm talking about is an inner trust, acceptance, and knowledge of yourself. Casting directors, agents, producers, and everyone else in the business generally aren't terribly concerned about your being the next Laurence Olivier. What they are concerned with is: Are you real, responsible, confident of what you can do and of your limitations, relaxed, dependable, and pleasant to work with and talk to, and of course whether you have the look and quality they happen to be looking for. Time and time again friends of mine have told me how they've gotten a job when they least expected it. Usually that's because they had gone to an interview or an audition not really expecting to get the part (which is not to say they were unprepared!) and were so relaxed that their natural qualities and abilities came out to their best advantage. Their attitude was *professional*, and most importantly, professional in a natural, relaxed way.

So go in there and have a good time and be yourself. And get to know the secretaries and receptionists. You need all the friends you can find in this business. Indeed, one of director Adrian Hall's assistants told me Hall used to pop into the outside office after interviews and ask his staff, "OK, who was an asshole outside?" You wouldn't want to be named on such an occasion, would you?

## AUDITIONS

Auditions are the means by which the stage actor and the beginning film or TV actor show what they can do. If you are at the beginning of your career, it is absolutely essential that you learn to audition, and to audition well. An audition is, of course, an artificial situation; it's a form of acting, of course, but it's not acting in a play (or a film), and it's not, in most cases, acting with other people (much less with costumes, scenery, and props). It often takes place without an audience, or in an empty studio, often in the most depressing of circumstances. It is thus only a fragment of acting, and often you feel fragmented doing it.

But you *have* to do it, and you have to do it well. Young actors (and old ones, too) often have hangups about auditioning and feel they audition much more poorly than they perform on stage or on camera. This, indeed, may be the case, but there's no use simply lamenting it. Producers with thousands of actors to choose from don't need to bother having faith in you. They will choose someone they *know* can do the role, and they will know it on the basis of that actor's audition. Even stars audition. Marlon Brando, about as big a superstar as existed at the time, auditioned for his role in *The Godfather.* Frank Sinatra auditioned for *From Here to Eternity.* Susan Sarandon auditioned for Annie in *Bull Durham,* "and let me tell you, it was humiliating," she reports. For live theatre, as actress Tovah Feldshuh says, "In New York, *everybody* auditions. They may not call it that. It goes under the guise of 'going over the score,' but it's the same thing. Directors like to see who they are working with."

So, learning how to audition—and to audition well—is a necessity.

You can audition either with a prepared monologue, a prepared scene for two persons, or a cold reading, depending on the circumstances. You can also be asked to sing, to improvise, or to demonstrate specific skills.

Dramatic monologues are fairly standard for stage work, and particularly for open calls; two-person scenes are sometimes used for film and television auditions. Stage auditions are usually in a rehearsal hall; film and TV auditions are most likely to be in a CD's or producer's office (and sometimes even a home or hotel room). You must be prepared for any combination of these variables.

In *open call* auditions, you will generally be offered the opportunity to present one or two monologues, ordinarily with a two- to five-minute time limit. If there is a singing audition, sixteen bars is the usual limit; the call will usually state if you are to sing *a cappella,* or bring an accompanist, or whether an accompanist will be provided (in which case you bring your sheet music). Sometimes you can bring your own accompaniment via a prerecorded cassette tape and cassette player; in this case, you should have it *precisely cued up* (allowing time to turn it on, put it down, and start singing), and you should *practice singing with it* many times before the actual audition.

Open call auditions are the "cattle calls" of show business; CDs may see twenty or thirty of you an hour (many more if it's a dance audition), and it's hard not to get depressed at the minimal attention you'll be getting, and the massive competition for that minimal attention. If you've seen *A Chorus Line,* you know what it's all about. That show was created by people who knew professional auditions from the inside out. Still, people do get cast from open calls, and persistence pays off. A UCLA master's student, Jim Birge, monitored 16,086 Equity Principal auditions back in 1981; these resulted in 155 actual work contracts, which is to say that almost 1% of those auditioning got cast. Elinore O'Connell, newly in Equity at the time of the auditions for the Los Angeles *Les Misérables* company, simply *knew* that Fantine was her role. She prepared her audition daily for months before the open call. But 3,000 actors showed up at the appointed date, and she didn't make it in the room on either of the first two days. On the third and final day of auditions, O'Connell arrived at the theatre before dawn, but found that hundreds of actors had camped out all night; she still couldn't get in. Undaunted, she asked if she could wait at the door anyway, in the hopes that someone wouldn't show up; well, everybody showed up, but a production assistant finally had some pity on her—and as the sun set over the Hollywood Hills, O'Connell was asked to come on in and sing. Yes, of course, she got the role.

Every actor should have prepared audition pieces always at the ready. You never know when you might get a chance to audition, and you should have a few pieces ready to go without thinking much about it. Often you will do a couple of prepared pieces not quite in the range of the parts being cast (how are you supposed to know?), and the director will ask "Got anything else?" or "Have anything funny?" Obviously, you should be ready to oblige.

For stage work your audition pieces should be monologues. Most LORT auditions ask for two contrasting monologues, one in verse and one in prose, delivered in no more than four minutes. Usually, one of these pieces should be something written before the nineteenth century, and one should be fairly contemporary. Graduate auditions through U/RTA should be in this format, also. Although it is rarely required that one monologue be from a comedy, it is usually quite helpful if one is— casting directors who may hear dozens of monologues in a three-hour casting session are ordinarily quite grateful for something that is genuinely funny, witty, or charming—among all the Medeas and Hamlets.

For film and television general auditions you should prepare scenes with a partner rather than monologues, and with a partner who will generally be available for fast-breaking opportunities that may arrive in the future. Choose your scenes and rehearse them carefully. In preparing auditions, you should keep the following in mind:

- *Brevity* is essential. If four minutes is specified as a maximum, that doesn't mean that three minutes and fifty-nine seconds is the minimum. Don't try to fill up the time frame; give yourself some elbow room, and deliver a real jolt: theatrical *impact.* Your audition should grab the CD's attention right away, tease and taunt a bit, build to a climax, and then end powerfully.

- The *grabber* is critically important: You might not be aware of it, but directors generally get hooked in the first few seconds—or not at all. They want to get dazzled, and dazzled fast. Remember, the casting people are not passive and objective educators, looking for flaws and readying academic "critiques"; they are producers, looking for someone who will capture an audience, entertain them, wring them out, and send them home—raving about the show to their friends. You have four minutes to prove to them that that's you.

- The prepared monologue or scene should show you in a role in which you could be cast *today.* Particularly if you are auditioning for a film or television role, do something very close to your age and personality, and something in a style as close as possible to the style of the part for which you are auditioning. If you are auditioning at a dinner theatre, it is silly to do a scene from *Othello.* Even if you played old ladies in college, you will not do them on Broadway, so don't give them your Aunt Eller until you are in your fifties.

- Choose audition material that is self-explanatory. In no case should you explain, before your audition, the plot of the scene or the characterization you are trying to convey. At most you should say the name of the scene and proceed. Choose scenes that don't require specific pieces of furniture, properties, or extensive movement—scenes you could present in a variety of locations and without bringing a suitcase full of production aids.

- Choose audition material that is not shopworn; stay away from monologue books, and try to find fresh material. This isn't always easy, of course, for what is fresh to some is passé to another. For example:

OMAR PAXSON:  I get tired hearing the same thing over and over.
            [Find] a couple of minor characters from Shake-

speare that no one ever does, like Launce and Crab from *Two Gentlemen of Verona.* I never hear that.

ERIC CHRISTMAS: There is a list of pieces that you hear so often you wish they wouldn't do them. For example, Launce and his dog Crab turns up all the time.

These contradictory words of advice, moreover, are from the same audition textbook! It's no surprise, however; what is old hat in one year, or place, is a novelty in other quarters.

- It is frequently rewarding to find and extract scenes from contemporary *novels* for audition material; chances are the dialogue is realistic and the scene fresh. Remember, they are judging *you*, not the material, and it doesn't have to be a masterpiece for them to like you doing it.

- Choose audition material that is *exciting,* that excites you and the people you can get to look at it. "What good is truth if it's dull and boring?" says Michael Shurtleff in his excellent book, *Audition.*

- Go *all the way,* emotionally, with your audition. There's no sense in holding back, waiting for a director to show you the way; unless you're cast, there will be no director. Don't overestimate how much CDs can see into your silences and private reveries; let your feelings and words come out where they can be seen, heard, and *felt.* Excite the listeners. "How strong should the reading be?" asks former *Dynasty* CD Gary Shaffer. "The exciting readings get the role," he answers. "From my experience, the closer you get to performance level in your reading, the better chance you have of getting cast. The person who cries real tears gets the job."

- *Preparedness* is, of course, critical. How much should you prepare? There is no easy answer to that question; you can be overrehearsed, but you can never be overprepared. Preparation is what gives you confidence and calm—it takes your mind off yourself and lets you concentrate on the business at hand. A relaxed preparedness is perhaps the most professional attitude you can bring to an audition. When George C. Scott first decided he wanted to become an actor, he decided to read for the leading part in a campus production. Getting a copy of the script, he memorized the *entire part,* word for word, before he had the audition. "They were flabbergasted, nobody had ever bothered to learn the part for an audition. I got the role." All too frequently actors refuse to prepare on the grounds that it will rob them of spontaneity, but it takes little objective contemplation to realize that spontaneity is the result of careful, not shoddy, preparation. And that sort of preparation is never wasted.

- Prepare your scenes under the *various circumstances* in which you may have to perform them. Rehearse on large stages and in small, officelike rooms. Rehearse with a "director" watching you, or try out your audition piece as often as you can in an acting class, at a party, in your home, or wherever you can get an audience of one or more to see you. Get used to performing amidst general inattention and extraneous noise. Rehearse and prepare your introduction to your scene, your transition between one monologue and the next, and even the "thank you" with which you conclude your audition. Obvious unpreparedness is instant death in a prepared-scene audition, for if you have not taken the time and energy to work on your audition, how can you demonstrate your willingness to expend time and energy on your part?

- Keep your scenes *loose,* and not dependent on any single planned "effect." Let the environment of your performance, whether it be office or stage, affect what you and your partner do. Preparation does not necessarily mean rehearsing and fixing every movement and gesture of a scene; some actors prefer to prepare the lines of a scene only, and leave the physical and emotional actions free and unrehearsed. This is particularly useful for film and television auditions, and in fact more closely duplicates the way these scenes would be shot professionally than conventional stage rehearsing would. Remember, in an audition the producer is not looking for a completed performance, but for your ability to act convincingly (and, when you have a partner, to *react* convincingly, as well).

- Choose for your acting partner someone you trust completely. He or she should be willing to give you the focus if it is your audition. You might respond by working up some scenes your partner can use for auditions. But no matter whose scene it is, you look better if your partner is good rather than bad, so never select a poor partner in the hope of looking good by comparison.

- If you are permitted, or required, to do two scenes, choose two that differ in tone and style rather than in age. Generally you are asked to do contrasting scenes, such as comedy and drama, or (particularly with stage work) classical and modern. Do not think of these categories as absolute, and do not worry too much about whether *Tartuffe* is funny or serious or whether *St. Joan* is modern or classical. The point is to get two differing scenes that show you off to your best advantage. If you are confused about what kinds of scenes they want, ask.

- Above all, choose material that shows you at your best, and do your best. Your *very* best. As Jon Lovitz says, "Move them: Make them laugh, make them cry, scare them." You don't want your audition scenes to be merely good: You want them to be *great;* you want them to be *terrific.* Choose material at which you excel, even if it means not doing exactly what they have asked for or what has been suggested here. The audition fails if you do not come off looking better than anybody they have seen that day, and a merely competent job with material you don't like is as bad as nothing at all. Have your agent, if you have one, preview your audition pieces and comment. If you are doing a full stage audition, by all means get a director to help you.

- In actually giving your prepared audition, *take the stage.* Take and claim your space. You may know from experience that you're likely to be interrupted sixteen bars into your song, or fifteen seconds into your monologue, but put that out of your mind. For those fifteen seconds or five minutes, dominate the stage you are on and make it your own, for if you don't trust yourself, why should they? Make it a great sixteen bars, a terrific fifteen seconds. Never look as though you're waiting to be cut off; want to go on, and on, and on!

- Can you use a prop? A simple but appropriate prop that you can keep in your pocket, and bring out at precisely the right moment, can humanize and give a lift to an audition, particularly in a modern piece. One actor reports losing a role in call-backs because of a very cleverly incorporated flash instamatic camera in his competitor's audition; "A brilliant and outrageous idea," our colleague reports, "but I was edged out by a *camera!*" Now you, too, can do some edging out.

- Don't look directly at the auditioners unless they ask you to, but direct your audition generally toward them, a little to the side or over their heads. Let them see you as fully as possible. Choose the characters you're speaking to, and "place" them out in the audience, not to your profile.

- In group auditions, where other actors are waiting their turn, you may find you have a tendency to play to your fellow actors in the wings, rather than to the producers out front. This is easy to understand, for although the other actors may be your competition, they are also your peers, and you may find them a more comfortable audience. Don't. This is the time to turn your back on the competition, as it were, and take the stage as your own. Cruel? No. You are not auditioning as part of an ensemble, but as an individual actor. They will be, too.

- *Dress* for the audition. It is not necessary, and in fact it is sometimes downright harmful, to costume yourself fully for the part you're reading for, at least during your first audition. But it is vitally important to *look the part,* drawing on clothing from your own wardrobe, or clothing that *could* be in your own wardrobe. If it's a western, by all means dig out your Arizona gear; if it's in a law office, grab your pinstriped suit. Don't go so far as to look silly on the street, and don't go all the way into period dress—it may make you feel uncomfortable, and will almost certainly make you look desperate. Look the part without looking like you're trying to look the part. Look like you *are* the part.

Jonathan Schaech, who played the John Lennon–type character in the 1996 film *That Thing You Do,* came to his audition as a rock musician from the early 60s, wearing a black skinny tie and a 60's haircut. Admired one interviewer, "It wasn't like somebody costumed you; it was your own choice and your own ability to distill the character for the purposes of the audition." "I was there to get the job, and to show that I knew Jimmy better than anybody else," Schaech replied.

- And *look* like a professional actor. That does not mean to look like a college actor. As a rule, college actors are poorer and dress in a more slovenly way than professional actors. This may be fine in college, but it doesn't cut the same figure off the campus. Let's face it: Professional CDs, producers, and directors make good incomes, have American Express cards, stay in good hotels, eat in good restaurants, and associate mainly with *employed* actors. They may be artists, but they are also adult businesspersons in a grown-up world. Regardless of what we might think of the artistic temperament, the lifestyle of most regional theatre directors (and for that matter New York and Hollywood casting directors) is fairly conservative, and fairly middle class. Ripped jeans, bare feet, and stained T-shirts just don't have the same effect at AEA studios, in Hollywood or New York offices, or on resident theatre stages that they do in the state university experimental theatre. You, of course, have every right to be yourself and dress as you choose, and people will rarely *think* they are judging you on the basis of your clothing (much less admit as much) but to "dress down" for an audition (even if you simply cannot afford to "dress up") can create a level of alienation that your audition may not overcome. The image of disaffected youth is not one that you want to project in a professional audition. Even if you seek to become the long awaited "next James Dean," you had better learn to be comfortable in adult attire. Actors and actresses are not looked down upon in the least for auditioning in fashionable dresses, handsome jackets, trendy sweaters, shined shoes, managed hairstyles, and sharp, contemporary outfits. These are not at all *necessary*, and they won't—by themselves—get you any roles, but they will lead you to a quicker and higher degree of rapport with people who, after all, dress more or less the same way.

- One final word on clothes: You must be completely *comfortable* in them. If you are only comfortable in tattered campus gear, then that's what you're going to have to wear, until and unless you get accustomed to something better. You can't worry about the way you look. Worry, of course, is murder.

- Get in the light. Stay in the light. Speak up and be heard.

- When you finish your audition, don't apologize for anything. Don't give any indication that you aren't proud of what you did. This is not a time for abject humility (nor, on the other hand, for cocky smugness); if it seems appropriate, you might ask if there's anything else the auditioners might want to hear. You should do everything in your power at this point to convince your audience that you love to audition, that you enjoyed doing this audition particularly, and that you'd be happy to do it again if they were interested. Confidence, after all, is part of what you're being auditioned for; your auditors are looking not only for talent and what is appropriate, but for personal stamina and a positive, professional attitude. Don't turn them off by grimaces or mutterings that convey your personal discomfort, and only show that you're not yet ready for professional work.

- Auditions and interviews are both *competitions,* and you must understand and treat them as such. You are being examined for your usefulness in an industry that wants to make money through your efforts. There are many competitors for every acting job; each, in effect, is put on a moving treadmill and passed in front of the casting directors and producers. It is your task to *stop the treadmill* and make the auditioners take notice of your individual value to their project. Whatever you can do to accomplish that, within the bounds of your own ability and—yes—ethics, you ought to know how to do, and be prepared to do.

## COLD READINGS

Prepared scenes are for general audition purposes; cold readings are for a specific job.

In a cold reading you are given a copy of a script, often a typed manuscript, and often only a "side," which is a portion of the text with just your lines and their immediate cues. You are then asked to read aloud for the producers, often with other actors reading the other parts. Or, you may read with a stage manager or with the director or producer. In a cold reading, you are going for a specific part, so you know that a part at least exists, and you haven't yet been ruled out for it. So, you're getting closer! If you are right for the role, you may just get it. Your goal is to be *terrific*.

There can be several rounds of cold readings: an initial one followed by any number of call-backs. After a certain point, union actors can get paid for call-back readings.

Your cold reading should be delivered just as your prepared auditions are: powerfully, professionally, and confidently. It should also be true to the text as written. As Broadway director Hal Prince (*Phantom of the Opera*) suggests, "The people who audition well come out, stand still, read the lines as they appear on paper—they don't ad lib changes, they don't improvise, they don't swallow their lines into their sleeves because they object to being there in the first place. I don't know of another way of getting a job in the theatre."

A cold reading need not be entirely cold, and if the idea of cold readings frightens you (and it should), there is plenty you can do about it. Ordinarily you can read the script beforehand, perhaps in the office waiting room. Arrive early. For film and TV shows, SAG contracts provide that you can get the script twenty-four hours ahead of time. Sometimes this just isn't possible: The script may still be in the writer's computer—or mind. But ask, and be prepared to drive across town to pick up your side (your portion of the script), or see if you can have it faxed to you—there are services that will do that for a reasonable fee. Make no mistake about it, if you can memorize your part and make some terrific character choices ahead of time, even if you're not asked to, you're miles ahead of those who can't, or haven't. This is no time to hold back and waiting for someone to tell you what to do. It's your opportunity to *show* what you can do. "The casting director and the people he works for want you to be fully prepared for this call. . . . Often the actor who best understands the role and is securely off-book will land the role," says *Back Stage West* columnist Thomas Mills. "If you expect to wing it at the audition, your results will almost always be dismal."

But even if the script is thrust into your hands moments before the reading, you will have a chance to give it a quick skim. Try asking a question: for example, "Is this guy a wimp or what?" Or "Do I really fall in love with him?" You might be shy of asking, but most directors and producers are happy to talk for a minute or two about what they want, given the chance. Don't ask multiple questions, or seek to initiate any lengthy discussion, but it might help to know the character's basic age, social standing, and specific goals in the scene before tearing off into your reading. It will at least buy you a moment to scan the part and make some bold choices. Try to phrase just the right *specific* question (not "What do you want here?"), and then let the director help you out.

Don't worry if you can't pronounce certain words or if you muff odd lines. Nobody expects a polished performance at a cold reading, and no directors (no good directors, anyway) care at this point for absolute perfection of detail. What they are looking for is the essential character, and your basic theatricality in the role. Do you understand the part? Will you? Will you be sympathetic? Will you be exciting? Sexy? Entertaining? Will your presence *improve* the part, flesh it out from what lies there silently on the page? Are you going to be fun to work with?

If you excite them with your reading, and they feel you can learn what you have to learn between now and dress rehearsal, or the first take, you're in the running. If, on the other hand, you get flustered because you mispronounce the name of a foreign city or a character's name, your preoccupation with this lapse will ruin your reading, even though you may be the only one who noticed.

Your auditors are looking for *acting* skills, not reading facility. So *get your eyes off the page as much as you can.* Don't be misled by the term "reading"; the less you have to look at your script, the less you actually "read" it, the better you will be able to approach performance level, and a performance is, after all, what they're ultimately going to want from you. One useful trick is to keep your finger on the script at the proper place, and to "spot-memorize" a phrase or sentence at a time, so you can deliver your words while looking at the (real or imaginary) character you are addressing. Then, when you are ready to turn back to the text, your finger will point you to the next line to spot-memorize. In any event, never get buried in the pages before you. They want to see your eyes, they *want to see you see.* They want to see *what you see.* Always remember that you are demonstrating your ability to act, not to read.

If you can keep (or otherwise acquire) a copy of the script, do so, then memorize the part for any call-backs.

Intensity, persuasiveness, sexual longing, passion, madcap inventiveness—these are wonderful qualities to show in a cold reading, where they are appropriate to the material (and only you can judge what's appropriate), and maybe even where they are *not* appropriate. Blandness and passivity are the only true crimes in this medium. But it is best to avoid any broad external characterization in a cold reading, unless you are certain that this is what is absolutely demanded by the part and the producer, and unless you can do broad external characterizations extremely well. Read the character as yourself—as your most intense, exciting self—to the greatest extent possible, and let the director see your basic personal qualities and idiosyncrasies through your acting. If the role requires a dialect and you can do it perfectly, do it; if you can only fake it, don't try. In general, don't try *anything* in a professional audition that will make you look less than wonderful, unless they ask you to.

The reading will end when the casting director has ruled you in or out: "in" meaning "in at least through the next round of call-backs." Often, however, a director will be ambivalent or uncertain. You aren't exactly asked to leave, but you can tell that the director isn't entirely satisfied; no decision has been made yet. This is a good time to ask, "Excuse me, but do you think in this scene Martha should be a little sexier?" (Or "bitchier?" or "more compassionate?" or "funnier?") You might get a chance to do it again, and in a manner closer to the director's concept. If you get coaching, put it to use. This is not the time to debate or disagree, but to deliver!

You can work on your cold reading technique, of course, in the privacy of your home or in specialized classes. Tony Barr, CBS producer and founder of the Film Actors' Workshop, advises that "you should work your tail off learning to become a good cold reader. Your career will probably hinge on it. Take a speed reading course. At the very least, read aloud from any source whatsoever for at least fifteen minutes a day, taking your eyes off the page as much as you can without interrupting the flow of your reading."

Sometimes in an audition or an interview you will be asked to take off your clothes. Contemporary films frequently involve nudity, and so, from time to time, does contemporary theatre. There are strict union regulations regarding this, and you should be aware of them. It is entirely proper for a director to get some idea of what your body looks like, and you might be asked to show your shape without having to undress. Under no circumstances, however, may a director ask you to undress without having informed you *when the appointment was made* that the part involves nudity and that you will be asked to disrobe during the audition. This at least gives you time to check out the producer and make sure you know what you are getting into. Union rules also require that you may bring a *friend* to the audition in these cases.

Remember that your agent and the union (even if you are not a member) will protect you from unscrupulous voyeurs who happen to be producing films and plays. On the other hand, if you plan to do nude films or plays, you had better plan on doing nude auditions as well.

You will have to adopt a pretty stable audition attitude. Like everything else in the life of a beginning professional actor, auditions can lead to paranoia. Even if everybody from the producer on down is extremely polite, you are nevertheless unceremoniously directed to perform when they ask you and to leave when they tell you. Frequently you are ushered onto a stage and see nothing in front of you but bright lights and a few shadowy forms at the back, and you hear nothing but "Name!" "Well, let's see it!" and, in the middle of your prepared monologue, "Thank you very much. Next please!" It is discouraging to the strong and ruinous to the weak, and you had better be prepared for it. A professional attitude is your point of strength. Remember always that you have to stop the audition treadmill. Only if you are solidly confident can you be strong enough to do that.

## THE SCREEN TEST

Screen tests are still sometimes used in Hollywood to see how you look on camera. The screen test may be a very simple affair whereby you turn your face from left to right in front of a camera and speak some lines or improvise a conversation. Or it can be as involved as a complete scene that you rehearse with a studio director and perform with sets and costumes. For major roles in films and television series, the screen test is usually the last stage of the audition, and the finalists for a certain role may screen-test opposite each other. Only newcomers are ordinarily screen-tested, however, since veteran actors can be seen by studio executives in actual film or taped performances available to them on call.

Screen tests are not as common as they once were; on the other hand, videotaping of auditions has become routine, especially in Hollywood, and it is virtually universal in commercial casting. It has even become common for stage auditions. Videotape allows a director to hang on to your audition for a while, to show it to other people after you've left the office, and to examine you closely and repeatedly against other contenders for the same role. It is wise to study camera-acting, and to work with videotaping equipment, as preparation for your career. There are numerous commercial schools, advertising regularly in the trades, that offer both instruction and facilities for taping auditions and scenes, and you should explore these opportunities.

## SOME OTHER OPTIONS

Thus far we've been looking at acting in the "big three" of commercial stage, screen, and television. But there are several acting options you might consider that fall a bit outside of that basic triangle. These include performing in TV commercials (a big moneymaker), in industrial shows, on a cruise ship, on CD-ROMs, on voiceovers, in student films, or as an extra.

## TV Commercials

Commercials are staple income for many actors between their dramatic roles; some actors, indeed, work in the commercial field exclusively. The top pay is outstanding when it comes: It is not unusual for an actor to make five to ten thousand dollars from a single national commercial—if it runs successfully. Indeed, commercials are the single biggest source of income for SAG performers, who picked up nearly half a billion dollars for such work in 1995—more than in either films or television.

National commercials, which are the only real money-makers for actors, are mainly cast and produced in New York or Los Angeles, with New York still slightly ahead in the volume of production. In recent years, Chicago has proven an up-and-coming "third city" in this field, and now accounts for about 10% of the national action. Local commercials are shot in cities around the country. Specialized agencies handle most of the casting and production for this mini-art form.

Rounds, interviews, and auditions for commercial work follow pretty much the same pattern as their counterparts in film and television work, except there is more of everything—more rounds, more interviews, more photos, and more pavement pounding. Commercial actors are always "on the street," often with garment bags in their back seat or over their shoulder, for the work is rarely more than a day at a time, and there's tremendous competition for each little part. A union card is essential for commercial work, but you can get on the street without one, armed with a *Ross Reports* (in New York) or with one of several studio guides in Los Angeles.

Commercials don't always use all of you. There are specialists in this field—"hand" people, for example, who are never seen but from the wrist outward, usually holding the product in a provocative manner. Honey-tongued speakers can "audition" by making *audio* demo tapes for voiceovers; these are the voices that speak off-camera, narrating or bringing home the message of the commercial. Many professional studios will make such demos for you (they advertise in the trades), and agencies will listen to them. "The most successful people in this business," says a commercial producer, "knock on doors and send tapes. They apply themselves. With talent and application you've got to make it in this town [Los Angeles] because this town soaks up talent."

Virtually everyone admits that acting in commercials "is not acting." In fact, some of it is deliberately "bad" acting, by normal standards, so as to "burn in" (an advertising term) the sponsor's message all the more forcefully. "Ring around the collar! Ring around the collar!" You might feel better about it if you considered acting in commercials as acting in a 30-second Bertolt Brecht "theatre of alienation" play, where your goal is not to create a convincing character, but to convey an idea (OK, to sell a product) to the audience. It's an alienating role, that's for sure. "We have no names," laments one commercial actor, "we're just the 'talent.' 'Send the talent out!' they call. They never even ask your names." "It's demeaning," says Linda Kelsey (a commercial actress who has graduated to starring roles in prime-time TV). "It's kind of plastic acting—instead of selling the truth of a character you're playing, you sell the fantasy of the product." But it is lucrative work, it is honest work, and you meet a lot of people on their way up too; today's commercial director is very likely tomorrow's film director. Commercials also get your face on the screen, often in L.A. and New York, where it counts. Sandy Duncan's professional career took off with a California bank commercial, which, although shown only locally, gave her great visibility in Los Angeles; without that commercial she wouldn't have played Peter Pan in Peoria. And Rob Fitzgerald, who finally (after more than a hundred commercials) became famous as Bud Light's "I love you man" guy, hadn't even landed a film/TV agent until he sobbed for his suds in the 30-second format.

If you go for commercial work, go for it fully, and respect the work for what it is. "Never, for a minute, feel superior to it or treat it with disdain," writes Cortland Jessup. "Don't waste your time passing judgments or getting caught up in the 'is it acting or not' debate." Commercial work requires bright spontaneity, strong discipline, and improvisational skills. "I use the same technique to learn a 60-second spot as [to do] Neil Simon," says Beverly Sanders, one of the finest performers in the field. "The key to me in commercials is to listen. You must be a quick study, and you must pay attention to the director, to *everyone*. It really takes a good actor to do a good job." It took Sanders eighteen months of foot pounding to get her first commercial, but now she has done hundreds of them and has made it her career. You may wish to try it only part-time, if at all. If you do, go into it with a full commitment.

There are many classes in both New York and Hollywood–Los Angeles on commercial acting technique (they advertise in the trades), and there are also a couple of worthwhile books on the subject listed in the appendix.

## Industrial Shows

Industrial shows (sometimes known as "business theatre") consist of stage productions mounted by corporations or industries that are, more or less, the "commercials" of live theatre—though a great deal less frequent. Over a hundred producers across the country produce these shows, which are presented at dealers' conventions, buyers' conventions, and other in-house gatherings of corporations or national groups of various kinds. The industrial show can be based around a theme, or used to introduce a new product, or even to sing the praises of the corporation's management and history. Many of these shows are splashy mini-epics, produced with great professional skill, and on high budgets.

Performing in industrials usually demands first-class musical skills (singing and dancing); good stage credits are also highly desirable if not mandatory. The pay is excellent (it's Equity's highest minimum salary), the working conditions sometimes spectacular (you may perform in the Caribbean or Hawaii), and the duration is short, putting you back on the street before you know it, a little tanner and a lot richer. Almost all business theatre is packaged in New York; you can get the names of producers from the occasional listings in *Back Stage* (the New York trade paper). The days of business theatre may be waning, however, and in 1995 actor work weeks (968) in industrial productions were only a third of what they were ten years before. Indeed, business theatre income accounted for less than half of one percent of Equity earnings in 1995, so you shouldn't be planning a career around it: Business theatre is quickly becoming no business, not show business.

## Performing on Shipboard

Cruise ships have become a relatively new performance venue since this book was first written. Mainly for singer/dancers, shipboard performance is increasingly remunerative at the financial level (since the salaries include room and board, and you'll have virtually no other expenses). Plus, it pays the added dividends of foreign travel and possible oceanic adventure for those capable of hitting their high C's on the high seas.

Most shipboard contracts are for six months, and, though non-union, pay at approximately LORT A wage levels (roughly $600 a week). You will, of course, have to both dance and sing, and you'll probably also be expected to entertain the clientele during the day: running bingo tournaments, teaching ballroom dancing, and hosting "What's Your Line?" games after dinner. You'll be required to "have a presence on the ship"; outgoing and unattached young performers are particularly recruited for these spots. You might enjoy this, and the learning experience—playing before large (if captive) audiences night after night—can be potent. Some of the ships have state-of-the-art stages comparable to top Vegas showrooms. Of course there is the occasional seasickness, shared (and cramped) cabins, and nightly parades of baba-rhums and baked Alaskas to put up with in the dining room. Auditions, if you're interested, are held regularly in New York and Los Angeles (they're advertised in the trades), often for casts of fifty to seventy-five at a time. Don't think you'll get in a Disney film just because you dance on a Disney cruiseship, but you're at least a half-step in the right direction.

## Acting in CD-ROMs

Or you can act on computers. Believe it or not, actors can make six-figure salaries in the CD-ROM market. Stars are particularly sought, of course. Christopher Walken and Burgess Meredith star in *Ripper* by Take 2 Interactive Software; between them, the actors received a reported $1 million of the CD-ROM's total $4 million budget for this one. "I wouldn't want to make a living doing it. But I would do it again. They paid well, and they were very jovial, and it was all a lot of fun," said Meredith. But regular actors are increasingly finding this an active field. Walter Koenig, who played Pavel Chekhov on *Star Trek,* now plays in *Maximum Surge,* a computer game.

## Voiceovers

A voiceover is an off-camera voice; you hear them all the time in radio and TV commercials, some TV shows and films (the callers-in to the radio talk show on *Frasier,* for example), and in animated films, where the voiceover performer may have star status. Voiceovers are also employed in films that are made in the United States and, before being shipped abroad, dubbed into foreign languages. Voiceovers—both English and foreign—are also used in the diversified corporate video/CD-ROM field, which in recent years has expanded the voiceover field well throughout the country. While you're not necessarily likely to be the voice of the next Lion King, a lot of voiceover work goes to relative unknowns who have mastered this particularly challenging art.

The techniques of voiceover performance are daunting, but—for most actors—learnable. You have to be able to speak with great clarity, particularly in the CD-ROM field where audio quality is not up to broadcast standards. You have to be able to speak rapidly and with high energy, especially in animated films where you have to make seeming emotional transitions (for example, from furious to terrified) at, well, Donald Duck speed. You should be able to do a variety of voices— wacky cartoon characters as well as persuasive advertising pitches and inspiring public service announcements. For film voiceovers, most producers will want to hire you for a virtual repertory of characters: say, three roles for the price of one. You should also learn dubbing ability —which is the skill of reading your script and looking at the screen at the same time, blending your words with the character's lips. If you want to do foreign language dubbing—a burgeoning field as the film world grows increasingly international—you must ordinarily be a genuine native speaker of the language, and sometimes even a native speaker of the character's regional dialect.

You can train for voiceover work at several specialized schools in the Los Angeles and New York areas; the schools should also get you aimed toward the best current career tracks in this field. Lots of agents and casting offices specialize in voiceovers: Your calling card to them is not a photo but a high-quality, professionally-produced demo tape, about three minutes long, with ten to twelve different voice samples. While union actors (SAG/AFTRA) will get the bulk of production studio work, most corporate and foreign production companies employ nonunion performers. The pay—which is usually by the day or the hour—depends on many factors: your union status, the depth of the producer's pockets, the specific supply/demand ratio of voiceover artists in your area (French dubbers get paid more than Spanish ones in Los Angeles, for example), and, in TV commercials, the length of time your voiceover is on the air—for voiceover artists in TV get residuals along with the other actors. Voiceover pros may earn $500 to $1,000 a day in this field, though rarely with clockwork regularity.

## Student Films

You don't want to act in a student film, do you? Heck, you've *been* a student; that's all behind you now. Well, you might be passing up a great opportunity. Acting in a student film at one of the nation's top film schools—such as the acronymic pantheon of NYU, UCLA, USC— while it won't get you any money, can nonetheless provide, in addition to a terrific on-camera learning experience, some solid (if semi-professional) resume credits, great clips for your demo reel, and real industry contacts—particularly if your director or cinematographer goes on to bigger and (commercially) better things. You might even be making great cinema art: That, after all, is usually the intention. Dustin Hoffman, Bridget Fonda, and Alec Baldwin all acted in student films. Robert DeNiro's first film role, in fact, was in *The Wedding Party,* a comedy that took four years to complete, two more to release, and received disastrous reviews. But it was directed by Brian de Palma, then at Sarah Lawrence, and the rest—as I suppose you've heard—is history. Indeed, a great many American directors went to film school and made such films, and they remember the actors who toiled for nothing in them.

Student films are advertised in the trades, and the roles are sometimes put out by Breakdown Services. Often they are technically quite sophisticated; some even get national distribution. You're rarely paid anything for participating in a student film, but you'll be offered CCM —which stands for copy (VHS tape), credit (cast billing), and meals (usually Domino Pizza). Your copy, of course, depends on the film's being completed, which only about half are (many run out of funds or energy, or the student graduates or drops out). And you might get paid after all. Many student films (about forty a year) are produced under a SAG experimental contract, which provides for deferred compensation (at least to the SAG actors) that kicks in if the film ends up being distributed commercially. Even if you're nonunion, you'll probably be able to negotiate for some of those proceeds as well.

## Write Your Own

Of course, with the right talent, application, and persistence, you can write your own play or screenplay, and write yourself into it as well. And, indeed, sometimes you can win the double jackpot. The most famous—nay, legendary—example of writing oneself into a starring role is surely Sylvester Stallone, who wrote the screenplay of *Rocky* when he had only played two small roles in Hollywood. Stallone offered his screenplay with the proviso that he play the title role; producers, though admiring the script, insisted on a name star for the lead. Stallone held his ground. Though broke at the time, he turned down offers of up to $200,000 for the script, until United Artists agreed to his terms; you know the rest. More recently, hard-plugging Hollywood actor Jon Favreau, while between supporting role engagements, wrote a script about himself and his actor-friends, and eventually produced it as an independent film—with himself and his buddies in the leads. Released by Miramax in 1996, *Swingers* swiftly escalated Favreau's and his friends' acting (and now writing) careers. Nothing in all this should suggest that it's easier to break into show business by writing than acting—and of course it is said that everybody in Hollywood is working on one or more screenplays—but writing your own show can surely put one more iron in the fire.

## Be an Extra

Everything has changed in the past few years with "atmosphere players" or extras, as they're commonly called. Standard advice in the past was to steer clear of this work, which meant playing nonspeaking parts in feature films and TV, on the grounds that being an extra forever typed you as a nonactor. 'Taint so anymore, and for one main reason: the disappearance of the Screen Extras Guild (SEG). Extras now come under the jurisdiction of SAG, if they come under union jurisdiction at all. Needless to say, this has gone a long way to remove any onus that might have adhered to being an extra.

Here's how it works: Each show (film or TV) that needs extras must contract a certain number of SAG members (currently fifteen in TV and thirty for a film); beyond that they can cast as many extras as they like. SAG members seek extra employment through a variety of specialized extra-casting agencies (such as the famous Central Casting agency in Burbank); nonunionites may apply for extra work the same way, although several extra-casting agencies are union only. (Central Casting is union only, but it has a nonunion division, known as Cenex Casting, which is in the same building but down the hall.)

To work as an extra, you sign up with an extra-casting agency. They keep you in a file—with four or five thousand others—which they can make available to casting directors, producers, and directors, often by CD-ROM. More commonly, you will call your agency's "message line," which is a daily recording of what's available: This is a day-to-day business. If there's something that suits you, you can call in to the agency's call-in line and, if you get through to an agent, get booked. Once you are better known at the agency, you might be invited to call in on an agent's private, direct line. You can also hire a calling service to make these calls for you—for a fee. You can find names and addresses of several extra-casting agencies in the appendix, and even more in *Working Actors Guide* or similar books available at drama bookstores in Hollywood. Most will ask you to apply in person; some accept photo-resumes instead. Nonunion hopefuls can submit snapshots in lieu of 8 × 10s; Central Casting demands proof of U.S. citizenship. The best extra-casting agencies charge no fees (they get their commission from the producer) and are selective in taking clients; others may charge nonunion types a modest $50 or so, and take anybody who shows up. All may levy a small charge for retaking or digitizing your photo for the CD-ROM.

Why should you consider extra work? Not to support your family, certainly, unless you work into the way wee hours. Nonunion extras currently (1997) make the munificent sum of $40 a day, based on eight hours, which doesn't quite make it up to the minimum wage (though it probably will by the time you read this). Union extras make $86 for the same day (as of July 1997). Both union and nonunion extras make time and a half for the first four hours of overtime, double pay for the next four hours, and their daily rate *per hour* for what's called "golden time" after that. Plus you can get "bumps" of from $5 to $50 for various extras: wearing your own formal garb, using your car, operating firearms, and so forth.

But if money isn't a major reason for doing extra work, experience might be: There's surely no better way—apart from actually getting an actual acting job—to learn your way around a Hollywood studio or film location. Moreover, you can—if you're not so brazen about it as to get kicked off the set—meet some of the people there too. One of my former students, Edmond Stoops, signed on as an extra for the film *Meteor* and spent most of his down time chatting with the star (and his idol), Peter O'Toole. When in one scene O'Toole needed to address a line to someone, he turned and said it to Stoops. The director, a bit taken by surprise, indicated that Stoops should respond, which he did; ergo, Stoops was in SAG—as well as a luncheon partner of Lawrence of Arabia.

And there's another reason to do extra work these days, as discussed under "Unions." Hang around the assistant director, and if the SAG minimum for the day doesn't fill, the AD's got to give somebody those SAG contracts (they're called "SAG vouchers"), and it might as well be you. Get three of them, and you're in the union as well.

Extras do go on to be actors. Sissy Spacek's first role was as an extra on Andy Warhol's *Trash;* she had one second of screen time. Mel Gibson earned all of $20 for his first film, *Summer City;* he earns $20 million a pic now. Sylvester Stallone's first part was as a hooded gangster in

Woody Allen's *Bananas;* he had no lines and wasn't listed in the cast—
a small start for a giant career.


## THE JOB OFFER

If you have played all your cards right, if you are as good as you think
you are, and if your contacts, interviews, auditions, and cold readings
have gone well, you may be offered a part. You now have to decide
whether you will take it or not. For most actors, this is the easiest decision of their lives.

There are some jobs, however, that you might want to think twice
about taking, even if they are the first thing that comes your way.

The job could be a nonunion job. Many theatres and independent
film companies skirt union regulations and jurisdiction. Even though
they may pay you a union-scale wage, they do not operate according to
certain procedures that the union requires of all producers. Check
with the union. If the producer is operating in frank violation of union
regulations, you may find yourself blackballed from future employment. This is rare, but investigate. If it happens to you, you may never
live it down.

The job could be quasi-union. That is, it could be a workshop or
experimental production (some student films come under this category) that operates under a special waiver or dispensation from the
union. In such a case you may not be paid, or you may be given
"deferred payment," which means you will not get the money until the
project is successfully marketed. If the project is nonunion but operated in accordance with the union, you have nothing to fear from participation, but you might not get more out of it than the work itself.

The job could be union but far from the city (*any* city), keeping
you from auditioning for bigger things in the near future. You could
be hired, for example, at a summertime Equity dinner theatre in the
mountains, and while you're carrying spears and waiting on tourists,
you're also missing auditions for the next Broadway and off-Broadway
season in New York.

Or the job could require nudity. Or pornography. Please don't
confuse the two. It's been well demonstrated that acting in full-on
pornography—XXXX skin flicks and the like—is quite immaterial to
your long-term career, other than as a modest source of income (and
possible immodest infection). The days are over when careers could be
ruined by exposure of pornographic dalliances in the past, but we

haven't reached the point where your future will be exactly enhanced by it either. Stay clear.

But there is a great deal of nudity in more conventional theatre and film, which may mean revealing quite a bit more of you than you've prepared for. Distinguished Broadway hits such as *Passion, Angels in America, Love! Valour! Compassion!, Equus,* and the London prize-winner *Stanley,* plus the majority of "R" rated feature films and "M" rated TV cable programming employ frontal nudity for both men and women. Bared breasts and buttocks are increasingly seen even on network television programs these days. You may say that you will only do such a scene if it is "tastefully done"—but, naturally, everyone will assure you that "*of course,* it will be tastefully done," and the real problem is there is no way to tell what is meant by "tasteful" until the final cut or dress rehearsal. So you will simply have no idea when you take the role just what parts of you your mother will see when she goes to see you in it. At any rate, don't hold out hope that "if they want me badly enough, they'll get a double for the nude scenes." They probably won't want you that badly.

And doing nude scenes may be even harder than you think, even in films (where you might think you only have to do it once). If it were a matter of simply flipping off a robe, shooting a quick scene, and then dressing again, that would be one thing. More often, even for a simple ten-second shot, many hours of takes and retakes will be required. Yes, SAG rules require a closed set in such cases, but you still will find yourself standing, sitting, and lying around in the nude amidst fifty technicians, actors, and producers (all fully dressed, of course) while they take, focus, retake, and refocus your ten-second nude scene, taking coffee breaks in between. Strong, uninhibited actresses have been reduced to quivering tears by this dehumanizing process, which, after all, is exactly how the Nazis humiliated prisoners. Tovah Feldshuh turned down half a million dollars to star in the film *Exquisite Beauty,* finding that she was to be in the nude for forty pages of script; there are some things that money cannot and should not buy, and you might want to consider your own stamina for this kind of thing.

The role may be otherwise offensive. It may be pornographic, or the style of the material may be too clichéd and ridiculous for your taste and talent. You may be asked to work with actors or directors you do not respect, or in a television show you loathe. You may be asked to do a commercial for a product you find personally disgusting, or to do a dialect you find ethnically or racially degrading. The role, you may feel, may be too small.

The job could be a daytime drama. "What, me do a *soap opera?*" many actors have moaned. Sure, why not. Daytime TV is, at minimum, a great training ground for on-camera acting. "It's like being shot out of a cannon," says Jennifer Roszell of *Guiding Light.* Says Leann Hunley of *Days of Our Lives,* "You're getting paid to learn, you're thinking on your feet every day, and you do every range of emotion possible. It's like being in an acting class day after day, with not a week apart." A high school dropout named Demi Moore says that her best training came from playing Jackie Templeton on *General Hospital* back in 1982. The list of actors who've been on soaps will stagger you: How about Meg Ryan, Alec Baldwin, Luke Perry, Hal Holbrook, Charles Dutton, Roy Scheider, Robert DeNiro, James Earl Jones, Peter Falk, Cicely Tyson, Ted Danson, Kathleen Turner, Christopher Reeve, Morgan Freeman, Bonnie Bedelia, Christian Slater, Ellen Bursteyn, Warren Beatty, Larry Hagman, Kevin Bacon, Sigourney Weaver, JoBeth Williams, and Olympia Dukakis? A recent trend is for soap stars to go into Broadway leads, such as Michael Damian (*The Young and the Restless*) starring in the revival of *Joseph and the Amazing Technicolor Dreamcoat,* Ricky Paull Goldin (*Another World*) and Jeff Trachta (*The Bold and the Beautiful*) starring in *Grease,* and Paul Anthony Stewart (*Loving*) playing Christian in *Cyrano: The Musical.* Of course, these actors were trained for more than soap operas, but it was their visibility on daytime that made them more bankable for nighttime. Guiding Light: Since you've only got One Life to Live, don't turn up your nose at the Days of Our Lives; not As the World Turns, anyway.

## Take the Job

There are, then, a number of reasons why you might not choose to accept every job that comes your way, and why you might want to wait until the "right one" comes along. For every acceptance ties you up and holds you back from possibilities not yet known. But this is mainly cavil, isn't it? The veterans know this. Lucille Ball once said that the way she got to the top of her profession was by taking *absolutely every job* she could get. Tony Curtis was quoted in *Variety,* as saying, "I think anybody in this business should take any job he can get today." Jason Robards says, "The only advice I have for young people is, no matter how you do it, do it in front of people who pay." So unless you sense an utter and absolute catastrophe ahead, TAKE THE JOB. There is more than just an immediate reason for this: One job will lead to another, power begets power. One fine actor worked steadily for ten years, at which time he looked back and realized that *every single job* he had gotten (except the first) evolved out of a previous one. A beginning actor, therefore, should refuse a paying acting job only for extraordinarily compelling reasons.

## HOW MUCH WILL YOU MAKE?

You have a job. Now that you have struggled, humbled yourself, and suffered financial hardships by the carload, you are ready to cash in your chips, right? What will the job pay?

As we've made clear so far, the income of an actor is not great. But if you work you get paid, and you should know how much that will be.

All the unions have negotiated contracts on your behalf; these contracts specify, among other things, the minimum salaries you will receive. These salary "scales" are written in astonishing detail; the Codified Basic Agreement negotiated between the Screen Actors Guild and the various motion picture producers is a 172-page book. The contracts are renegotiated continuously upon expiration, so the following information, which is accurate as of this printing, is subject to regular change.

### Stage Roles

If you land a part in a Broadway play, or in the national tour of a Broadway play, you are covered by Equity's Production Contract. Your minimum weekly salary under that contract will be $1,000 a week in 1997, rising to $1,180 in the year 2000. If you tour, you'll get an additional $630 in expenses in '97, $700 by the millennium. The production contract covers barely more than a quarter of stage actors' annual working weeks, but more than half their annual income.

Get into an off-Broadway show and you'll make $469 per week in the company's main house, and $294 per week on its smaller second stage.

Regional theatres are classed in five salary groups—according to size and potential gross income—by Equity. LORT A theatres—such as Minneapolis's Guthrie Theatre, Los Angeles's Mark Taper Forum, and San Francisco's Actors Conservatory Theatre—paid a weekly salary minimum of $610 in 1997. For the same year, B+ companies like Princeton's McCarter paid $583, B companies like Atlanta's Alliance $563, and C and D companies (which are often the ratings of smaller stages in the larger companies) $536 and $446 respectively. Small Professional Theatres (SPTs) naturally, pay somewhat less, owing to their "developing" status. And Equity waiver theatres—the L.A. ninety-nine seat theatre plan—will pay you $5 to $14 per performance, probably not enough for a cab to the theatre and back again. Like production contract rates, these salary minimums will rise approximately 4.25% every year until the millennium.

Can you argue for more than the minimum? Well, obviously Broadway stars draw the big bucks: $30,000 to $50,000 weeks are in the ballpark. But the average Production Contract salary, commingling stars and walk-ons alike, was $1,477 per week for Broadway performers in 1995. And in most off-Broadway and many regional stages, the scale minimum is in fact the universal wage. So-called "favored nations contracts," common in those venues, provide that everyone gets the same scale pay and the same billing. It's resolutely fair, but fairly bleak as well.

If you are nonunion, of course, minimums don't apply. Apprentice actors can get $100 a week, or less, or more, or even nothing; it's really up to the theatre and the actor. Shakespeare festivals pay nonunion actors $2,000 or more for the summer—which might run for twelve to fourteen weeks. But then housing is often provided, and additional money may be paid for leading theatre tours and teaching classes once the shows are open.

The fact is that few actors can truly earn a living simply by stage work. Fewer than half of Equity's members worked at all in 1995–96. Fewer than 15% were employed in any given week. The median professional stage actor's income in 1996 was simply zero. (That's right: $0.00.) The median *working* actor only made $5,754.

"The situation for an actor in New York these days is that one can't afford to be an actor," says Paul Hecht, who has won Tony nominations and critical praise for his many Broadway and off-Broadway roles, but earns his living doing TV commercial voiceovers. "I don't even know what other job it's comparable to. And we're talking about people who are high up in their profession, not people just out of school. You're looking at a middle-aged man at the height of his artistic powers who has to treat [stage] experiences as if they were artistic sabbaticals. But I'm an actor, and I love the theatre, and I'm stuck."

## Film/TV

If you find employment in films or television shows, higher minimums prevail. Basically, in films you will be paid either by the day (as a "day player") or by the week; in television you can be paid by the day or week, or for a three-day half-week. The current prime-time dramatic television contract for SAG, also applying for AFTRA, will give you a minimum ("scale") of $559 for a day's work, and $1,942 for a week—at least in 1997–98. You'll also get your agent's commission on top of this, though of course you won't ever see it. (Thus you're paid, in industry parlance, "scale plus ten" or the minimum fee plus 10%.) And you'll get another ten bucks if you're asked to wear your own clothes, and $25 to wear your own tuxedo or formal gown. Expect all these figures to rise in future years.

Increments apply for recurring series roles. There's also a special three-day rate ($1,415) for TV shows, which will save the producer some money, and an "under-five" rate for videotaped shows under AFTRA contracts, for roles with fewer than five lines. You may also be an "under-five" (and not just an extra) if you are addressed individually by a principal performer or are alone in a scene, so long that you portray "a point essential to the story" and are provided "individual direction."

Salaries in soap operas are structured a bit differently. Starting salary for a daytime beginner—which is based on a $680 a day scale—actually averages, in 1997, between $750 and $850 an episode, with a guarantee of one and a half episodes per week (that is, 39 episodes in a 26 week cycle). A three-year contract is fairly standard, so this normally generates a genuinely livable income. A second year will bump you up $100 an episode, plus another half-episode a week; the third year bumps you another $100 and perhaps another half-episode; thus putting you well into a six-figure IRS bracket for the year. Experienced daytimers and daytime stars, naturally, make a *lot* more.

Television actors also pick up residual bonuses for subsequent reruns of their shows. Residual payments begin with an additional 100% of your actual compensation for any prime-time network rerun (up to a ceiling of $2,125 for a half-hour show, and more for longer ones), and then on a diminishing scale (from 50% down to 5% of compensation) for subsequent non-primetime network and/or syndicated reruns. There is also a provision for additional compensation for foreign telecasts at 15% to 35% of the applicable minimum, depending on various factors. Actors in TV commercials, in fact, can live off their residual checks. A single commercial, shot for a day's pay, can pay residual income for years, even decades: There are actors who've made twenty to forty thousand dollars for a single TV commercial shot in one day. That TV commercials run for years on an increasing number of broadcast and cable networks is why commercials provide more actor-income in our country than any other medium.

The potential for big salaries in film and television, of course, is huge. I mentioned the "$20 million club" at the beginning of the book, those dozen or so actors who command that amount per film. There are actors (Arnold Schwarzenegger is one, according to *Fortune* magazine) who've made as much as $50 million—that's enough to run your college drama department for the rest of your life—in a single year. Indeed, star salaries are now twenty to thirty times what they were when the first edition of this book appeared in 1972.

But featured players, particularly on TV, have not enjoyed such a boom time. "Scale plus ten" is increasingly considered close to the "top of the show" salary for guest-star or guest co-star TV roles, even for veteran pros who play them. Actors who were accustomed to $10,000 a week for a TV guest slot are now swallowing hard and signing for a $2,700 "top" on the same show (or, in exceptional cases, a "double-top" of about $5,500). That may sound like a lot of money for a week's work, but there aren't that many actual working weeks in a year for most TV actors, and five weeks at the "top" (which is a pretty good year for that sort of work) may not even pay the rent. Even recurring TV roles don't pay what they did even a half-decade ago. Starting salaries for series regulars have fallen as much as 75%: down from $30,000 an episode in 1993 on one leading show (it typically shoots twenty-two to twenty-six episodes a year) to about $7,500 in 1997.

Salaries for featured film roles have also not kept up with the salaries at the top. Part of the reason is that star salaries simply eat up the budget. Jim Carrey's $20 million for *The Cable Guy* was, as mentioned, about half of the entire production cost; it left little for everybody (and everything) else. This is not, to be sure, Carrey's fault; it's simply an economic fact of show business: "Bankable actors," which means those whose names will generate production loans, can "open" a film (put it into production); ordinary actors' names cannot.

And part of the reason, in Hollywood at least, is the influx of East Coast stage actors, coming from New York and Chicago, who aren't accustomed to working for—or asking for—the ten grand a week. "They're delighted to work [in films and TV] for $2,000 or $3,000," says one Hollywood agent. "It's making it very hard for actors to survive [here], and therefore harder for agents to survive."

The fact is, of course, that it's hard to make a living as an actor, even as a very good and very well-known actor, and even in films and TV. The work is uneven, unsteady, and unsure. Neither Tony nor Emmy nor Oscar awards mean there's necessarily a job for you next month, or next year. Even established stars are always hustling: Henry Fonda said, toward the end of his storied career, that getting work was his "operative problem. . . . You have no idea what your next job is . . . you think, 'Well, that's it! I won't work again!'" And if Fonda feels that

way, how do the rest of them feel? I'll say it again, in somewhat different words: Acting is a club, not a profession. There aren't 10,000 actors
in the country who will make a genuine living this year—the year
you're reading this—and fewer than half of them will make a living for
each of the following next five years.

## GETTING THE SECOND JOB

This book has focused on getting your first job. Getting the "big
break." Most young actors believe that the first foot in the door pries it
wide open. Unfortunately, this isn't so. The door can slam shut all over
again, and be even harder to open a second time.

Think this isn't true? Shakespeare festivals, which typically rehire
two-thirds to three-quarters of their designers and technicians for the
following season, rarely take back half of their actors. Why not? We
don't always know. Maybe they want their audiences to see fresh faces
on stage (they don't do the same plays, do they?). Maybe the non-
rehired actors didn't deliver on all of their artistic promise—not night
after night, anyway. And maybe, just maybe, those actors were simply a
collective pain in the ass.

Listen to veteran stage/film actor/director Charles Grodin: "It's
amazing to me how actors don't seem to realize that being troublesome will impact their careers. Working on the other side of it as a producer, director, or writer, I can say that the first question that comes up
when people are interested in hiring someone is, 'What's he like to
work with?' And word gets around quickly. Employers call each other,
and you definitely can get hurt if you cause people grief."

Your behavior on the set, in fact, is the second most important tool
of getting rehired. The first is delivering a knockout performance, of
course, but the second is hardly less important—at least when there
are others around who can also deliver knockout performances. And
there always are.

Listen to Jeff Greenberg, the veteran casting director for stage,
film, and television: "I want to hire wonderful people to take to a set
filled with wonderful people. I don't want an inkling of an attitude.
There are enough people out there that if there's someone we feel
might be troublesome, we just don't want to go down that road."

I think it's necessary to carry this a bit further than to just say,
"Behave yourself and don't be troublesome." What you really must do
is actively, vigorously, and even rapturously support, heart and soul and
then some, the production and production team that's been smart

enough to hire you. Actively. Passionately. Without reservation, moodiness, alienation, or the slightest hint of carping.

You think that's easy? No, it's not. There will surely be things to criticize or complain about if you're the type to do so. That's fine in the academic theatre. Indeed, it's expected, it's what "academic" means (the term comes from Plato's original teaching gymnasium). But it can spell disaster for a beginner in the professional theatre. Remember, Plato never had to deal with opening nights, howling investors, or union regulations. You've been hired as a professional, so be professional. Recall the words of screenwriter James Agate, "A professional is a man who can do his job when he doesn't feel like it." There will be times you might not feel like it; transcend them. "Acting professionally," the title of this book, has a double meaning: Think about it.

Prepare fully, and then even more fully, for your first day in the rehearsal hall or on the set. Make decisions about your character, your character's goals, tactics, expectations: Do everything you've learned to be outstanding from the first moment of rehearsal. If you can, learn your lines solidly, and then more solidly, even before rehearsals start, and particularly for work in film or television. "The single most startling principle to grasp for the theatre actor entering the world of film for the first time," says Michael Caine, "is that not only have you got to know your lines on day one, you will also have directed yourself to play them in a certain way. And all this accomplished *without* necessarily discussing the role with the director, *without* meeting the other people in the cast, *without* rehearsal on the set." And while stage actors normally have the opportunity of learning lines during, rather than before, rehearsal, don't take advantage of that. Rather, use line-learning *to* your advantage, and get to work on it immediately. In any event, you're not going to have the luxury of casual preparation you might have enjoyed back in school. Broadway director Jerry Zaks expects a full-out, word-perfect run-through two weeks into rehearsal. You (the beginner, presumably with a small part) should be ready in two days. If you really want a second job, that is.

And then, in the studio or on the set, deliver. Share. Be alert, ready, eager, capable, and professional. Don't waste people's time asking special favors, but make the most of every opportunity you have. Work for the success of the whole production, not just your little part in it. Help the other actors in any way you can. Michael Caine again: "Almost without exception, actors help each other. In the movie business, the list of people whose careers suddenly ground to a halt is the same as the list of actors who tried to make enemies or pull tricks." Be positive and courageous.

And be healthy! Acting, unfortunately, is simply not a business where you can just call in sick, even when you *are* sick. No note from your mother—or doctor—can repay the production company for the lost hours of rehearsal or shooting caused by your absence. A missed rehearsal—for whatever reason—can seriously jeopardize a stage production; a missed day on the film set could cost tens, even hundreds of thousands of dollars, even if you're not the star of the show. A reputation for chronic ailments is particularly deadly: No production company can mortgage the schedule to your migraine headaches or chronic fatigue syndrome. If you suffer such medical problems, you'll have to figure out how to work through them at maximum capacity when you have to. Or you should seriously consider another line of work—one where you are more easily replaceable on a day-to-day basis. "The show must go on" is more than a cliché; it's an economic necessity.

Do I really *have* to do all this?, you might ask. No, you don't have to. And nobody will make you. But you should. Not because I say so, or because anybody says so (and few people *will* say so, since nobody in this business wants to come off as a scold). Do it because you want to be seen not only as a *great* actor but also as an actor who has a *great attitude*. Not just a good one, not just an acceptable one, but a truly great one. Memorable. You should want people to be *dying* to hire you, not just willing to.

Get it? Good.

# Chapter 6

# Other Opportunities

If you've come this far, where are you?

You have talent, personality, contacts, training, a home base, a photo-resume, an agent, an interview technique, some knockout auditions, a union card, and now a first paying job.

You are at the beginning of your career. You know where to find out what you need from here on.

But a career is not merely begun, it must be sustained. That will require your constant attention, your every effort. Nothing comes easy to an actor, and nothing *stays* easy. The steps of the ladder are irregular; there are long gaps in between. And maybe when you get halfway up, you find the ladder isn't going where you wanted to go.

In this final section, take a look at some possibilities for acting professionally *outside* the established entertainment industries.

## OUTSIDE THE INDUSTRY

Everything in this book, so far, is about how actors accommodate themselves to the existing theatre, film, and television industries—which, of course, have their own rules and procedures, and some of which may not thrill you as you get closer to them. "You've got to really be *sick* to want to be an actor here," says a well-known Hollywood agent. To be an industry actor means to stand, sit, smile, and squat on command, and often the command comes down from a source that you are hard pressed to respect.

Industry acting means schlepping about at your own expense, from office to office, from casting director to casting director, and being emotionally and financially subject to a ruling elite in which you may have no personal interest or sympathy.

Industry acting means spending most of your life looking for work, even when you are well into middle age. And most of your professional concentration won't be on developing the work itself, but rather on developing your network of contacts, and figuring out where the next job is coming from. That's exciting, to be sure, but will it be so in the coming years and decades? And how will you feel at 40 years old, being asked "So, tell me about yourself, Charley" by a casting director half your age? How will you feel at 60?

When you must audition and interview regularly for work, when that work is rarely won—and is transitory when (and if) it comes—you may begin to develop psychological problems. After all, it is *you* that you are putting up there on the stage, and it is you getting knocked down over and over. When rejection is piled atop rejection, no matter how many successes come in between, something happens in the pit of your stomach. Insecurity nibbles at your psyche, anxiety saps your nerve. Every job you lose must mean a personal flaw. You may retreat into a shell and self-destruct, or you may stuff yourself with bluster, and become a parody of your former self. Actors who defensively over-inflate their egos, promoting their talents and sounding their trumpets upon the least occasions, become the most pathetic sights in New York and Hollywood. As the fine actor and director Austin Pendleton points out:

> Nothing bothers casting people more than the neurotic oversell, and that is because an actor who oversells himself is an actor who does not trust himself and nothing, *nothing* disturbs show business professionals more than that. Self-mistrust is, after all, the ulti-mate buried nightmare for anybody in the business, as it is for bullfighters and tightrope-walkers.

Are you a bullfighter or a tightrope-walker? Most actors fight con-trary desires warring within them: a desire for security versus a lust for fame; a desire for personal happiness versus a need for artistic and emotional freedom. Many industry actors, even successful ones, find themselves virtual slaves to their profession, and are unable to make a personal decision without first consulting their agents, their produc-ers, and their managers. Others enslave themselves to a set of industry conventions that are brutally dehumanizing. The vast majority are poor almost to the point of starvation. You can see why your parents paled when you told them you wanted to be an actor.

More and more people today are seeking, and finding, acting careers outside of the acting industries. These careers must be called compromising for those who seek solely to act for a living—they ordinarily require additional tasks and tangential skills—and they don't ordinarily offer even the distant hope for superstardom or superwealth. If you are utterly committed to being a professional actor, you will probably find these quasi-acting careers unacceptable, and, for the truly committed actor, they probably *are* unacceptable. But you should take the opportunity to think about them, and about yourself as well, before heading off into the industry.

## COMEDY AND SOLO PERFORMANCE

Stand-up comedy was one of the growth industries of the 1980s; at the beginning of that decade there were only a handful of professional comics, mainly filling spots on the *Tonight Show* and working the occasional Las Vegas or New York nightclub—and by the decade's end there were more than 2,000 pros working in 370 full-time comedy clubs around the country, appearing on dozens of talk/interview TV shows and a twenty-four-hour comedy cable network, and, for that matter, teaching most of the driving-safety programs authorized by California's Department of Motor Vehicles. By the 90s, many of those club comics, indeed, have become actors—mostly on TV sitcoms, but also in films—and even serious films. A partial list of ex-comics now acting professionally would include, at minimum, Steve Martin, Billy Crystal, Richard Pryor, Ellen DeGeneres, Eddie Murphy, Drew Carey, Garry Shandling, Brett Butler, Jon Lovitz, Roseanne, Robin Williams, Bill Cosby, Tim Allen, Dante, Jon Stewart, Margaret Cho, Paul Reiser, Richard Lewis, John Mendoza, Jerry Seinfeld, Greg Giraldo, Ray Romano, and Kevin Pollak. "Isn't it time that TV abolished affirmative action for stand-up comics?" asked Harold Rosenberg in the *Los Angeles Times* when reviewing Giraldo in *Common Law*.

Let's add to comedy the art of solo performance (the "one-man" or "one-woman" show), which today includes some of the most brilliant theatre artists of our time: Eric Bogosian, Sherry Glaser, Jeff Weiss, Claudia Shear, John Leguizamo, Lily Tomlin, and Lori Anderson. This genre, which often cross-lists with performance art, normally does not begin in any wing of the world-wide entertainment industry, but strictly in the imagination of the artist. Often it moves into the realm of off-Broadway theatre (Sherry Glaser's *Family Secrets*) or Broadway theatre (Jackie Mason's *Politically Incorrect*), and sometimes into film acting (Bogosian's casting in *Under Siege*); but solo performance—like comedy—is an art in itself, not merely a break-in opportunity for the industry. It may appeal to you strictly for its own, considerable, rewards.

Comedy and solo performance can be an outstanding way to develop stage presence, make friends in the world of entertainment, and pay the bills. It is also, as we've seen, a great stepping stone to the stage or studio, if that's your ultimate goal. Of course, you will need an inventive wit, an original style, a uniquely perceptive view of the world around you, and gigantic quantities of self-motivation and ambition: Neither comedy nor solo performance gives you a playwright or director who might offer guidance or encouragement. But if you have (and can deliver) the goods, and that's a big "if," put together a knock-out act. Comedy, in particular, is a relatively easy field to break into, and you don't need scenery, a partner, or a role to audition for. Most clubs find time to look at new talent occasionally (some have an "amateur night" or an "open mike" night), and you can at least get seen without too much ado. Getting seen by Dave or Jay or their talent scouts, however, requires more exposure than a single shot at your local club, so you will have to build up a repertoire of routines, and a repertoire of clubs you perform in, in order to move up the ladder.

## ACADEMIC THEATRE

A second alternative is academic theatre. America doesn't yet have a national theatre, but we do have a series of publicly supported theatre and film-producing units in the nation's colleges and universities. These theatre, drama, video, and film departments, which began as academic branches of English, speech, and communications before (and shortly after) World War II, have become producing organizations that, within their obvious limitations, advance live theatre, and film and video art, in exciting ways. Hundreds of professional theatre artists now associate themselves, both part-time and full-time, with academic drama and film programs, partly for the financial security and prestige such positions can bring, and partly to have the freedom to work without commercial limitations.

A position with a university drama or film department will generally require you to *teach* acting—and/or directing, playwriting, filmmaking, dramatic literature, or theatre technique, usually for a nine-month academic year. This can leave you free to act professionally at summer theatres, and some institutions may offer some of the contacts to help bring this about. You may also be in a position to direct plays with students, and perhaps to act in student productions as well. Depending on the institution, you may have a high degree of freedom to teach and direct material you choose, and in a manner you choose. Academic employment in this form provides a reasonable annual salary and, at most institutions, a position with eventual job security (tenure) if you make the grade. Professors at the top of their profession can earn sizable salaries (over $100,000 for a nine-month academic year at some places) and move in some interesting circles, including professional theatres.

Academic life also provides an intellectual fervor, a great measure of artistic freedom, the excitement of working with young people, and, at some institutions, occasional sabbatical leaves (in addition to summers off) with full pay. Some institutions also run professional theatres, with faculty artists hired as the situation provides, thus giving you a chance to enjoy the best of both worlds.

But university theatres and film schools are academic, not professional, arts institutions, and any academic position entails a compromise of the highest professional standard. If you find daunting Shaw's famous phrase "He who can, does; he who cannot, teaches," know that it will echo in your mind throughout your teaching career.

An academic position, as you would expect, requires far more in the way of intellectual and pedagogical preparation than does the ordinary Broadway or Hollywood or LORT career. University jobs are *not* easy to come by, nor are they easy to sustain. Many universities demand that their drama faculties publish books or articles in their areas of specialty (the well-known "publish or perish" formula), and all serious academic theatre departments require their staff members to develop and maintain active careers, either as scholars (evidenced by publication) or as professional-level actors, directors, or theatre artists (evidenced by successful artistic works both on and off the campus). The best institutions also demand excellent teaching, as evidenced by sound and innovative pedagogies (teaching plans and theories), students who look good on stage and get work when they graduate, and good teaching evaluations. A successful academic career, therefore, is every bit as professional and as demanding as the acting careers we have heretofore been discussing.

If you are interested in pursuing a career in academic theatre, you should *at minimum* earn an M.F.A. degree from a highly reputable institution—the best that you can get into. If possible, seek a Ph.D. as well. Choose a field of interest and read everything you can about it; develop some new ideas of your own. Learn one or two foreign languages, particularly as they may be useful in your field of interest. Attend scholarly conventions (the Association for Theatre in Higher Education—ATHE—is the umbrella organization in this area), and find out how you can make an artistic or intellectual contribution to future conventions. You will make your strongest job application by developing a professional reputation along with your academic one. Write and publish some scholarly essays or play reviews, or establish yourself as a director or actor with a summer theatre, LORT theatre, off-Broadway theatre, or other professional group. Write plays, or translate them, and get them produced. Make a name for yourself *somewhere*, for there are literally hundreds of applications for every drama faculty opening, even at institutions of modest repute, and your application needs the cachet of something special besides your academic degree and your splendid faculty recommendations.

The job market for drama faculty aspirants is year-round, but most positions begin in September, with the application period beginning the previous fall. Openings are widely advertised by law (how refreshing, for readers of this book), and you should check the monthly listings in *Joblist*, published by ATHE (P.O. Box 15282, Evansville, Indiana 47716; you must join the organization first to get a copy), and the twice-monthly *Artsearch*, put out by TCG (355 Lexington Avenue, New York, NY 10017). If your training and interests are more on the literary side, you should also check the positions listed by the Modern Language Association (MLA). ATHE holds a national convention every summer, where you'll find a number of last-minute academic posts available to ATHE-registered jobseekers.

Successful university drama and film instructors are invariably people who have a love for teaching, for academic freedom, and for the university life. Teaching, on the other hand, may be a very unhappy alternative for the person captivated by the wish to act professionally, or who is intellectually insecure. A university instructor is simply not a professional actor or director, but a professional educator, and would-be actors who go on to graduate school only to get a degree "to fall back on" may never find much satisfaction on a college campus. Essentially, an academic program is still one of scrutiny and analysis as much as it is of production and performance. Academic life is fascinating to anyone driven by curiosity and a desire for knowledge; but it is a supreme bore for someone looking only for the thrill of the follow-spot or the film studio. And, as it involves as much effort to become a successful professor as a successful actor, it cannot be recommended that a budding actor expect to "fall back" on the profession of teaching. You will probably only fall back on your back.

## YOUR OWN COMPANY

For the performer who wants to create and perform, but has little or no interest in academia, there is a third alternative between the industries and the campus, and that is the private, nonunion theatre company. Some of the most exciting and artistic work in America and abroad has, in the past, been done by such "amateur" companies, under the leadership of such near-legendary figures as Konstantin Stanislavsky, André Antoine, Jacques Copeau, and Jerzy Grotowski; and such moderns as Ronnie Davis, Robert Wilson, Paul Sills, Joseph Chaikin, Charles Ludlam, Julian Beck, and Andre Gregory. Such work is going on today as well; you may already know of a theatre collective or experimental group in or near your own town.

Such works often flower into full-blown professional operations, if that's what their directors wish. David Emmes and Martin Benson, together with several fellow graduates of San Francisco State University, created a tiny amateur theatre in an abandoned dockside warehouse in 1964—twenty-five years later, their South Coast Repertory Theatre had won the national Tony Award for regional theatre and was heading into the next century with Emmes and Benson still at the helm, and a half-dozen original acting company members still actively employed. Three of my University of California students from the 1960s crossed the continent after graduation to found the Lexington Conservatory Theatre in New York's upper Hudson Valley; that company's direct descendent, the Capital Repertory Theatre of Albany, is now one of the country's finest small (class D) LORT enterprises. Yet another student in their same class went north, founding the Ukiah Players and subsequently the Marin Shakespeare Festival, both thriving to this day. Talented and dedicated enthusiasts cannot only create theatre, they can create theatres in which to do it.

Amateur theatres begin and operate outside the established unions or industry. Some such groups may have a short life, to be sure, but some develop an enviable measure of security. Many are communal in both art and living arrangements. Most of these groups try to make ends meet at the box office, some survive with local or foundation grants, and some thrive for a generation or more without ever going under union auspices. Some—let's go all the way here—tour the world and create theatrical history: That's certainly true of Julian and Malina Beck's Living Theatre, Ronnie Davis's San Francisco Mime Troupe, and the Chicago Steppenwolf Company.

There's nothing to prevent you from looking up and joining one of these groups, if they will take you, and there's nothing to prevent you from starting up your own. All it takes is a building, some friends, some paint and plywood, and some energy and ideas. And ideals. True, you will have to work in the daytime at "regular" jobs in order to be free to rehearse at night, but if you are doing what makes you happy, you will be well rewarded. For most people, the urge to perform need not be satisfied by working on Broadway, in Hollywood, or on the Yale Drama School stage; it could be quite satisfactorily fulfilled by acting with friends before a small audience in your own home town. You should certainly consider this option before you pack your bags for either coast. Some of the most genuinely artistic work in the country is done at theatres like these.

As is true with the theatre, so it is true with film. The rapid growth of independent filmmaking in America in recent decades has been extraordinary, and a large group of nonunion amateur filmmakers is growing up nationwide. They have a literature, a character, and an opportunity to exchange presentations. Student and amateur films are being commercially marketed, too, so that a venture into independent filmmaking does not necessarily cut off all professional possibilities.

Television is entering a new age of decentralization that, at this point, holds even greater promise of diversified development. Camcorders and videocassettes, as well as the commercial availability of home recording systems and studios, augur an international flow of televised production that may or may not be professional in character. Video art is a recognized new form of expression that has been shown increasingly in museums and galleries during the past decade, and is developing commercial possibilities, even for actors. Local and national cable programming is now a new market for video art and videodrama, and dozens of companies are now entering the field of satellite distribution of original and rebroadcast television programming. "Superstations" now broadcast nationally and internationally, and airwave deregulation has permitted various experiments in specialized telecasting.

What does this all mean? Overall, it means less network and massmedium television production; and more local, specialized, and innovative production, providing new potential for close-to-home training, employment, and creative artistry in the video-acting arts. So the Hollywood connection is not your only track to a professional career in video performance. Your camcorder and a few friends might provide a start.

## OTHER THEATRE JOBS

Finally, you should be aware of the tremendous number of jobs in the theatre that are less visible than acting, but more widely available. Some of them you are probably quite familiar with: director, designer, technician, playwright, and stage manager. Others are described in the previous pages: agent, casting director, producer, production assistant, publicist. Chances are you haven't studied these professions—no courses exist for them in most colleges and universities—but they are, in fact, significant career options for thousands of persons trained in drama. There are far more jobs in these areas than for actors, and far fewer people clamoring to break in. There are even areas where the demand for talent exceeds the supply.

Such employment, of course, can lead to professional acting further on, if you're still game to get on stage. It may also lead to things you find you like even better than acting. Even very successful actors—Ron Howard, Diane Keaton, Clint Eastwood, Tom Hanks, Kevin Costner, Cher, Robert Redford, Rob Reiner, and Barbra Streisand are good examples—found a career change into directing inestimably rewarding at a certain point. Writing, casting, and producing are also where a number of ex-actors wind up, and they're usually very happy to be there. Some actors happily sit out the "middle years" of their adult lives in such positions, and then return to acting in their senior years. Casting director Burt Remsen, acting teacher Lee Strasberg, and director/educator John Houseman enjoyed stunning success as actors long after establishing themselves as masters in other mid-life career positions. Acting is one of only two professions in which you can start out—and rise to the top—wholly during your later life (being president of the United States is the other, as an ex-actor proved).

# Appendix

I have resisted the temptation to provide a list of agent and casting director addresses below, although they're very easy to come by. It takes about a year for any book to come out, from the time of its drafting to its appearance on the bookshelf, and in that year 10% of the phone numbers I would list here would already be out of date. There's no business as volatile, as rapid in turnover as show business. Is there another business whose standard directory is revised *monthly* (the *Ross Reports* flags more than 100 address or personnel changes each issue)? And no business is as susceptible to the ups and downs of hits, flops, blockbusters, and turkeys that change the status of its participants overnight.

Besides, freshly updated lists of addresses are readily available, for free or for nominal amounts, when you will actually need them. And they can be obtained in convenient packages, such as in preaddressed mailing labels, or in geographically coordinated "mapped-out" listings.

Therefore, the appendix to this book is an attempt to list some reasonably permanent *sources* of up-to-the-minute information that you can tap with a single visit or phone call.

I've also, for the most part, left out exact prices. The costs of services mentioned in this book have tripled or quadrupled since the first edition, and will no doubt continue to rise as rapidly. Indeed, the price of *this* book has more than tripled. Inflation has hit the labor-intensive acting industries as hard as or harder than it has the country at large, and the theatrical capitals, New York and southern California, are inflation leaders, as anyone who has tried to stay in a hotel in either town well knows. But the prices for the materials listed here are all reasonable; all the listings books, for example, should cost about the same as a movie ticket or two at the time you read this. The general trade books (which are bigger and more expensive) will cost about what similar books cost in other fields; so you may want to read them in a school or public library.

## WHERE TO GO FOR PUBLISHED INFORMATION

In New York, you can find virtually any material published about acting (or the theatre), including plays, books, journals, and trade papers, at the legendary Drama Book Shop at 723 Seventh Avenue, NY 10019 (that's catty-corner across the street from the Broadway TKTS booth, in the heart of the theatre district); they're on the second floor and open seven days a week. You can call them at 212/994-0595 or 800/322-0595, or fax them at 212/921-2013; if you know what you want and have a credit card handy, they'll be happy to take your order by phone or fax—even by mail. If you're further uptown on the West Side, visit Applause Books at 211 West 71st Street, NY 10023 (212/496-7511; fax 212/721-2856), which is just as extensive. Indeed, by all means drop by both stores when you hit the city; the personable employees of each of these delightfully welcoming havens are theatre buffs themselves—usually actors as well—and they'll be happy to offer you advice on the latest and best books on their shelves.

In Los Angeles, the Samuel French Theatre Bookshop at 7623 Sunset Boulevard (at the corner of Stanley) has everything you can imagine; in addition to being the West Coast outlet for the Samuel French catalogue of plays, it has virtually every theatre book and magazine in print, and a huge film collection as well. You can also order by phone from them at 213/876-0570 or 800/822-8669, or fax to 213/876-6822. Samuel French L.A. is closed on Sunday, but there is a branch at 11963 Ventura Boulevard in Studio City (818/762-0535) that's open all seven days if you don't mind hauling out to the Valley. An alternate to French's is Larry Edmunds' Cinema and Theatre Book Shop at 6644 Hollywood Boulevard, not far from Mary Pickford's handprints in the pavement; Edmunds' number is 213/463-3273.

In Chicago, it's Act I Bookstore at 2632 North Lincoln (312/348-6757); in Toronto, it's Theatre Books at 11 St. Thomas Street, 800/361-3414; and in Seattle, it's The Play's The Thing Drama Bookstore at 514 East Pike Street, 206/322-7529. Visit any of these spots when you're new in town; some will have flyers of what's happening in the local theatres, some two-for-one discount coupons to local plays, and even notices of rooms for rent. You'll also quite possibly run into someone you know—and almost certainly someone you will soon know; if actors constitute a family, these drama bookstores tend to be the kitchen table.

Maybe you want to sit in a comfortable library and read from a great collection of acting books. If so, there are two wonderful places for you. In New York, it's the Library of the Performing Arts in Lincoln Center (upstairs is the magnificent Theatre Collection of the New York Public Library, which has clippings from America's earliest theatre days). In Los Angeles, it's the Margaret Herrick Library at the Academy of Motion Picture Arts and Sciences (333 South La Cienega Boulevard, Beverly Hills). Both are free. The Library of the Performing Arts is open daily except Sunday, and the Herrick Library is open Monday, Tuesday, Thursday, and Friday. The Herrick Library emphasizes the literature of film (this is the academy of the Academy Awards), but there are plenty of materials on all the other media as well.

## TRADE PAPERS

You read the trades to know what's going on. But there are different types of trades: those primarily for producers and executives, which consist in the main of reviews, deals, and box office grosses; and those primarily for actors, with extensive casting information and advice. There are also a few specialty trades and magazines. You can find all of them at the theatre bookshops mentioned above, and most of them at newsstands throughout midtown Manhattan and Hollywood/Beverly Hills.

### FOR PRODUCERS AND EXECUTIVES:

*Variety:* published weekly in New York; international coverage of all media.

*Daily Variety:* weekdays in Los Angeles; primarily film/TV.

*Hollywood Reporter:* weekdays in Los Angeles; primarily film/TV.

*Theatrical Index:* weekly in New York; theatre.

### FOR ACTORS—these are the "trades" referred to in the book that will have full casting information in each issue:

*Back Stage:* weekly in New York.

*Back Stage West:* weekly in Los Angeles, with some duplication of its New York sister.

*Drama-Logue:* weekly in Los Angeles.

*PerformInk:* biweekly in Chicago.

**SPECIALTY TRADES AND THEATRE MAGAZINES—these don't have regular casting information, but survey their particular scenes in depth:**

*Latino Heat:* bi-monthly in Los Angeles; news of/for Latino actors.

*Black Talent News:* 10 annual issues, Los Angeles; some background casting information.

*American Theatre:* monthly in New York (TCG); news of regional theatre, but no casting information.

*Entertainment Weekly, Premiere,* and *Movieline;* national monthlies with news and gossip about actors, mainly in film/TV; no casting information.

## LISTINGS BOOKS

Whatever else, actors need a bunch of names and addresses and phone numbers to get around. While technically just about everything you will need is in the telephone book, that's a bit hefty to carry about on interviews. Moreover, the yellow pages won't tell you who runs the office, whether they see newcomers, and how to get through to the people that matter. The following listings books will do all this, and are regularly updated. New York and regional stage listings tend to be updated annually—these folks don't move around all that much. Hollywood and film/TV listings are updated more regularly, monthly in some cases, and some even have updates between months. All the listing books are available at the drama bookstores—and very few other places. But then you won't have much use for them in other places.

(Also note: There's a very high turnover in this field of quasi-literary endeavor; several of the listing books noted in the last edition no longer exist, and a few of those listed here may not exist next time. But the publishers listed below seem to have cornered the market and show longevity.)

**MONTHLIES (or nearly). Three publishers dominate the fast-moving updated-more-than-once-a-year market:**

1. Silverscreen Publishing (Acting World Books) puts out a series of large format, typed-and-photocopied paperbacks that cover

the entire Hollywood acting scene. Their listing books, which are very informative, chatty, and up to date, include:

*The Agencies* (bi-monthly, monthly update)

*The Casting Directors* (bi-monthly)

*Personal Managers*

*Acting Coaches and Teachers* (quarterly)

Silverscreen also published dozens of actor-help books (for example, *The Right Agent, The Film Actor's Complete Career Guide*) in the same, right-off-the-computer format. Prices average about $10 per volume.

2. Breakdown Services Inc., Hollywood. These are nicely published little pamphlets, listing L.A. addresses and phones without all the gab.

*The CD Directory* (CDs are listed alphabetically and geographically; published every three months, with inter-issue updates)

*The Agency Guide* (lists agencies and the agents within them; semi-annual, with monthly updates)

Very accurate (these are the same folks who get cast breakdowns from CDs and pass them on to the agents; they obviously know everybody in the business) and complete.

3. *Ross Reports*. Published in New York, but available on both coasts, these are highly authoritative and official vest-pocket-sized booklets you can carry around with you.

*Ross Reports: Television* (monthly)

*Ross Reports: USA* (a listing of agents and managers around the country)

There's also, for those interested:

*The Stand-Up Comedy Directory*, put out monthly by Velvis Productions in Los Angeles.

**AND YEARLIES (or nearly). The best comprehensive book in Los Angeles is:**

*The Working Actors Guide*, edited by Karin Mani. A 500-plus page compendium that lists (and, for the most part, describes) every agent, CD, theatre, film studio, photographer, acting coach, video lab, health food store, and massage service in the L.A.

area. Indispensable. Published annually in a spiral binding by Mani Flattery Publications in Studio City, California. Order by phone from Samuel French, Los Angeles (above).

And in New York:

> *The Back Stage Handbook for Performing Artists,* edited by Sherry Eaker. A book chock-full of career-oriented advice, together with 100 pages listing every agent and casting director in New York, Los Angeles, and Chicago; plus lists of personal managers; acting schools and teachers; cruise line, industrial show, and theme park producers; union offices; and most New York, L.A., LORT, and dinner theatres. Published by Back Stage Books in New York, and revised periodically. Out of town? Order by phone from the Drama Book Shop in New York (above).

And in Chicago:

> *Chicago Connection:* Everything the actor needs to work and live in Chicago. You can order this one by calling the publisher's office at 312/464-3230.

You may also find valuable actress/teacher K. Callan's excellent books:

> *The Los Angeles Agent Book*
>
> *The New York Agent Book*

These are chatty and informal annotated listings that go into detail on how to find an agent, how (and why) to fire an agent, how to talk to an agent, and so forth. Published by Sweden Press, and revised/updated periodically—about every two or three years.

For summer and regional theatres, the most authoritative sources by far are the following annual publications compiled by Jill Charles:

> *The Summer Theatre Directory*
>
> *Regional Theatre Directory*

Addresses for these books is P.O. Box 519, Dorset, VT 05251-0519 (telephone 802/867-2223; fax 867-0144). The formidable Ms. Charles is the Artistic Director of the Dorset Theatre, and is also the author of *The Actor's Picture-Resume Book,* available at the same address.

You will also find useful these two publications from the Theatre Communications Group (TCG):

*Theatre Directory,* an inexpensive vest-pocket pamphlet published annually, listing (in 1997) 317 nonprofit professional theatres in the U.S.

*Theatre Profiles,* a far more comprehensive book that details about 250 of these theatres, listing their officers and recent productions, indicating their goals and philosophy, with a production shot from each. Published in even years (volume 13 due in 1998).

## THE BOOK WHERE *YOU* LIST

*Players Directory* (Officially the *Academy Players Directory,* this is from the folks that sponsor the Oscars and operate the Herrick Library.) This is strictly for Hollywood-based film and TV. You can see the directory, and apply to get your photo into it, at the Academy headquarters, 8949 Wilshire Boulevard, Beverly Hills, CA 90211-1972; they'll only accept you if you are a member of an acting union, or a *signed* client of a SAG-franchised agency. You must classify yourself in one or more of eight categories: leading woman, ingenue, leading man, young leading man, male or female character/comedian, male or female child; if you want to list yourself in two categories (say, ingenue and leading woman), you'll pay double. You may list your agency representation(s) and/or your telephone service number, your guild affiliations, and up to six special skills and three professional credits. You can also be cross-indexed according to ethnicity (Asian, Black, Hispanic and Native American) or disability. Though few do, you can also indicate your height, weight, and age range. The *Directory* is published three times a year in four volumes (or one CD-ROM). The cost to list is currently (1997) $25 per issue and per category.

*Player's Guide.* The (somewhat) same thing in New York. Temporarily reorganizing as this book goes to press, but it will probably remain open only to Equity, SAG, or AFTRA members. Expected to be published annually in book and CD-ROM format.

## BOOKS ABOUT ACTING AND ACTORS

This is a select list of books you might wish to have in your personal collection, or read in a theatre library.

Alterman, Glenn. *The Job Book I, The Job Book II.* Lyme, NH: Smith & Kraus, 1995. Book I is acting-type jobs (such as game show contestant, role-playing in law school moot courts); Book II is standard day jobs—paper-hanger, and so forth. What to expect and how to get it.

Arlen, Michael J. *Thirty Seconds.* New York: Farrar, Strauss & Giroux, 1980. An amusing and insightful look into the making of a television commercial.

Babson, Thomas. *The Actor's Choice: The Transition from Stage to Screen.* Portsmouth, NH: Heinemann, 1996. Perhaps the best explanation of its subject available, with an excellent section on cold reading auditions.

Barr, Tony. *Acting for the Camera.* Boston: Allyn & Bacon, 1981. The best book available on film and television acting by a veteran actor, producer, and teacher.

Bayer, William. *Breaking Through, Selling Out, Dropping Dead, and Other Notes on Filmmaking.* New York: Delta Books, 1973. A stunning analysis of Hollywood from a unique point of view.

Beardsley, Elaine Keller. *Working in Commercials.* Boston: Focal Press, 1993.

Bremner, Belinda. *Acting in Chicago.* Chicago: Plays Inc., 1994.

Callen, K. *How to Sell Yourself as an Actor,* Third Edition. Studio City, CA: Sweden Press, 1996. Excellent advice from the author of *The Los Angeles Agent Book* and *The New York Agent Book.*

Cohen, Robert. *Acting Power.* Mountain View, CA: Mayfield, 1978; and *Acting One,* same publisher, 1984. An approach to acting, and an introductory text on the same theme, by the author of the current book.

Fridell, Squire. *Acting in Television Commercials.* New York: Harmony Books, Second Edition, 1986. Best in the field. Informative and cleverly illustrated.

Funk, Bob. *The Audition Process.* Portsmouth, NH: Heinemann, 1996.

Goldman, William. *The Season: A Candid Look at Broadway.* New York: Harcourt Brace Jovanovich, 1969. A candid and acid look at the Broadway theatre; still pertinent.

Grodin, Charles. *It Would Be So Nice If You Weren't Here.* Random House, 1990.

Hagen, Uta. *Respect for Acting.* New York: MacMillan, 1973. A gentle and instructive book on acting written by a fine actress and teacher; particularly interesting because it shows the way a New York actor thinks as well as acts.

Henry, Mari Lyn, and Rogers, Lynne. *How to Be a Working Actor,* Third Edition. New York: M. Evans and Company, 1994. A book not unlike this one, with lots of good information. Ms. Henry is a casting director, Ms. Rogers an actress, and their writing is lively and informed.

Hooks, Ed. *The Audition Book.* New York: Back Stage Books, 1996.

Lakein, Alan. *How to Get Control of Your Time and Your Life.* New York: David McKay, 1973. One young New York actor describes this as an *absolute* must. It may help you achieve a *professional* attitude.

O'Neil, Brian. *Acting as a Business*. Portsmouth, NH: Heinemann, 1993. Excellent basic coverage of the field.

O'Neil, Brian. *Actors Take Action*. Portsmouth, NH: Heinemann, 1996. Addendum to the above, with some strong pro-active tips on furthering your career.

Saint Nicholas, Michael. *Your First Year in Hollywood*. New York: Alworth Press, 1996. Comprehensive coverage of the L.A. scene.

See, Joan. *Acting in Commercials*. New York: Back Stage Books, 1993.

Shacter, Susan. *Caught in the Act: New York Actors Face to Face*. New York: NAL Books, 1986. Interviews with Christopher Reeve, Kevin Kline, John Lithgow, Edward Herrmann, Tom Hulce, William Hurt, John Malkovich, Raul Julia, Harvey Fierstein, and forty-five others, all men.

Shurtleff, Michael. *Audition*. New York: Walker and Co., 1978. An outstanding book, not only for its advice on auditioning, but for its general information about the acting process.

Silver, Fred. *Auditioning for the Musical Theatre*. New York: Penguin, 1988.

Silverberg, Larry. *Top Qualified Acting Coaches: New York; Top Qualified Acting Coaches: Los Angeles*. Lyme, NH: Smith & Kraus, 1996.

Small, Edgar. *From Agent to Actor*. Los Angeles: Samuel French, 1991.

Sonenberg, Janet. *The Actor Speaks*. New York: Crown, 1996. Twenty-four penetrating interviews with major contemporary actors, including Lily Tomlin, Dianne Wiest, Stephen Spinella, John Turturro, and Mercedes Ruehl.

You should be aware that there are a number of "junk" books on the market that purport to tell you how to break into the movies, leap onto the stage, or turn into a star in three easy lessons. One (*How to Get into the Movies* by Diane Morang) advises: "After interviewing with as many agents as you can, make a decision as to with which agency you would like to sign."

## UNION OFFICES

### NATIONAL OFFICES

*Screen Actors Guild*
5757 Wilshire Boulevard
Los Angeles, CA 90036
213/954-1600

*AFTRA*
5757 Wilshire Boulevard
Los Angeles, CA 90036
213/461-8111

(Note: Los Angeles offices of SAG and AFTRA are in the same building, but not—prior to merger, anyway—in the same space. SAG is on the seventh and eight floors, AFTRA on the ninth.)

*Actors Equity Association*
165 West 46th Street
New York, NY 10036
212/869-8530

**REGIONAL EQUITY OFFICES**

There are also regional Actors Equity Association offices.

*West:*
6430 West Sunset Boulevard #700
Los Angeles, CA 90028
213/462-2334

235 Pine Street
San Francisco, CA 94104
415/391-3838

*Midwest:*
203 North Wabash Avenue
Chicago, IL 60601
312/641-0393

## SCHOOLS OF THEATRE AND ACTING

There are nearly 200 graduate programs offering some form of professional actor training, usually at the M.F.A. level, and there are more than 1,000 undergraduate programs where acting is part of a general B.A. (or A.A.) degree in drama or theatre arts, or a more conservatory-style B.F.A. (Bachelor of Fine Arts). How to find information?

Jill Charles, *Directory of Theatre Training Programs,* regularly revised, is the best single listing of the M.F.A. programs in the United States (and a few similar programs in Canada and England). Available at drama bookstores, or at P.O. Box 519, Dorset, VT 05251-0519. (Call 802/867-2223 for faster service.)

There are also rankings of some of the country's more prominent programs—though the ratings are hardly scientific, and represent general reputation more than site-observed evaluation—which you can find in two books available at larger college-oriented bookstores around the country:

*ARCO Performing Arts Major's College Guide* (ranks both graduate and undergraduate programs as "most highly recommended" or "noteworthy"; regularly revised).

*U.S. News and World Report: America's Graduate Schools* (ranks twenty programs—intermixing M.F.A. with some B.A. and B.F.A.— numerically; appears each spring).

You can also get information on the thirty-one M.F.A. programs in the University/Resident Theatre Association, all accredited by the National Association of Schools of Theatre, by writing to U/RTA, 1560 Broadway, Suite 903, New York, NY 10036 (212/221-1130); e-mail: URTA@aol.com.

In addition, there are pages of advertisements from (and feature stories on) various drama training programs in several theatre magazines, including *American Theatre* (particularly), *Stage Directions, Dramatics,* and *Theatre Journal.* These journals, along with the ARCO and *US News & World Report* surveys, can be found in most college libraries as well as theatre book stores. *Back Stage* and *Back Stage West* also publish an annual guide to college performing arts programs as a pull-out insert each November.

There are also acting schools—and private coaches—not associated with colleges or universities, at least a thousand of them at last count, mostly but not all in the L.A. or New York areas. Check the listing books for a representative list, but a few of the most famous (by dint of their age, their size, or the importance of their founders) are:

*Lee Strasberg Theatre Institute*
115 East 15th Street
New York, NY 10003
212/533-5500
*and*
7936 Santa Monica Boulevard
Los Angeles, CA 90046
213/650-7777

The late Mr. Strasberg was long identified as the director of the famed Actors Studio in New York and became the principal progenitor of the American "Method" school of acting derived from the teachings of Stanislavsky.

*The Stella Adler Conservatory of Acting*
419 Lafayette Street, 6th Floor
New York, NY 10003
212/260-0525

*and*
6773 Hollywood Boulevard, 2nd Floor
Hollywood, CA 90028
213/465-4446

The late Ms. Adler began acting in the Yiddish theatre in New York. Meeting Stanislavsky later in Paris, she returned to set up a variant to Strasberg's Method—truer to Stanislavsky's vision in her view—which was based on imagination.

*Neighborhood Playhouse School of the Theatre*
340 East 54th Street
New York, NY 10022
212/688-3770

Founded by the late Sanford (Sandy) Meisner.

*HB Studio*
120 Bank Street
New York, NY 10014
212/675-2370

Founded by the late Herbert Berghoff, and now directed by his famed widow, actress Uta Hagen.

*The American Academy of Dramatic Arts*
120 Madison Avenue
New York, NY 10016
212/686-9244
*and*
2550 Paloma Street
Pasadena, CA 91107
818/798-0777

America's oldest dramatic conservatory, established in 1884.

You might also check out the programs of one of the newer guys in town (New York); this is

*The Actors Center*
12 West 27th Street, Suite 1700
New York, NY 10001
212/447-6309

Founded by J. Michael Miller in 1996, the Center brings together leading faculty members from Julliard, Yale, New York University, and the New York professional scene (Uta Hagen, for example) to offer a variety of acting programs and master classes.

Remember, however, no school is any better than its weakest teacher, who could be yours. The size, age, and national reputation of a school is far less important than the quality of instruction you actually receive in the classroom.

## EXTRA CASTING OFFICES (LOS ANGELES AREA ONLY)

A partial list; these places will all see new applicants. Call for drop-in hours, which are usually limited to a few hours per week. Bring a photo, proof of citizenship.

*Central Casting (union only)*
1700 West Burbank Boulevard
Burbank, CA 91506
818/569-5800
*and*

*Cenex Casting West (nonunion)*
1700 West Burbank Boulevard
Burbank, CA 91506
818/562-2888

*Hollywood Casting Inc. (union and nonunion)*
6253 Hollywood Boulevard #917
Hollywood, CA 90028
213/856-9070

*Rainbow Casting (union and nonunion)*
12501 Chandler Boulevard #204
North Hollywood, CA 91607
818/752-2278

# Index

student films, 139
supply and demand, law of, 7
Sylbert, Paul, 40

Taft-Hartley Act, 95
talent, 12–15
telephones, for actors, 73–75
termination, of agency contract, 101
theatre bars, 50
Theatre Central, 50
Theatre Communications Group
    (TCG), 57–58
Time Warner, 5
trade balance, U.S., 5
trade papers, 48–49, 163–164
training, of actors, 27–36
TVQ, 17
type, physical, 19–27

unemployment, of actors, 3–4
unions, 93–98
university training, for actors, 27–33
University/Resident Theatre Associ-
    ation (U/RTA), 66

voiceovers, 137–138

Walken, Christopher, 55
Walker, Nicholas, 29
William Morris Agency, 103
Wilson, August, 22
Winters, Shelley, 47
Witkin, Francine, 6
women, casting of, 19–22

Zaks, Jerry, 150